STRATEGIC CASE STUDY KIT

NOVEMBER 2012 AND MARCH 2013

V – TRAVEL BUSINESS

CIMA

BPP
LEARNING MEDIA

Sixth edition October 2012

ISBN 978 14453 9732 0 (text)

ISBN 978 14453 9288 2 (e-book)

British Library Cataloguing-in-Publication Data
A catalogue record for this book
is available from the British Library

Published by

BPP Learning Media Ltd
BPP House, Aldine Place
London W12 8AA

www.bpp.com/learningmedia

Your learning materials, published by BPP
Learning Media Ltd, are printed on paper
sourced from sustainable, managed forests.

Contents

BPP
LEARNING MEDIA

Question index

All questions are for 50 marks and should take 90 minutes to answer, excluding reading time.

Introduction

CIMA has made available, in advance of the Strategic exams, Pre-seen material for the Section A Question 1 case study on the three Strategic papers. This Pre-seen material is the same for all three exams at each sitting.

On the day of each exam, CIMA will provide **additional Unseen** information about V – Travel Business, the company featured in the Pre-seen. This information will differ in each of the three exams. When answering Question 1 in each exam, you should not include details from the Unseens in other papers in your answers. It is probable that most of the detail you will need to answer the requirements for Question 1 of each exam will be included in the **Unseen** material.

Using your BPP Learning Media Kit

This kit contains the following material:

- **Advice on how to use the Pre-seen to pass Strategic level examinations.** This is the first level at which assessment is conducted using Pre-seen material. You need to know how to ensure your exam scripts make best use of this material.

- **An analysis of V – Travel Business Pre-seen.** Our analysis includes a brief description of the industry in which V – Travel Business operates. We provide a section-by-section review of the Pre-seen material, highlighting important issues and areas that could be developed further in the Unseen material. However, you should remember that the Unseens could introduce new issues that are not mentioned at all in the Pre-seen.

- **A reprint of the V – Travel Business Pre-seen.** Between now and your exams you must gain a good knowledge of this material. You may have to draw on this material to support your answers in the three exams, so you should familiarise yourself with its layout by reading it over frequently.

- **Practice questions.** We have included four Unseen questions and answers for each of the three Strategic papers. These allow you to practise answering exam-style questions before the exam. Attempting these questions against the clock will help you develop planning and time management skills. The questions and answers for each exam cover different areas of each syllabus and include a range of question requirements. However, they are **not comprehensive** and you should expect to see **different situations and requirements** in the exams. **Do not** learn the answers in this kit and reproduce them in the exams. You must answer the questions set.

Using the Pre-seen case study to help pass Strategic Level

The Pre-seen case study sets the context for Question 1 on each of the 3 Strategic Level examinations. Each question is compulsory and carries 50 marks.

It is written by a management accounting academic with considerable experience in industry and as a CIMA examiner. It is written in consultation with the Strategic level examiners. The Examiners will derive some of the issues in their Question 1 from the Pre-seen case.

Understanding and using the Pre-seen, with the help of the analysis and simulation questions provided by BPP in the following pages can help you to gain marks in three ways:

- Greater familiarity with background and issues and technical content

- Deeper analysis of problems presented in the Unseen material on exam day

- Better illustration of benefits and implications of the recommendations you make

Familiarisation with background and issues

CIMA provides this before the exam to give you more time to read it and to get properly to grips with the firm and industry.

1. Your marks will be improved by coming to the exam day with:

2. *A clear idea of the Strengths and Weaknesses of the firm.*
   You should be able to back these up with examples and calculations.

3. *A general assessment of the Opportunities and Threats in the industry as a whole.*
   These will be obvious in the Pre-seen. You don't need to trawl through the trade media and internet to find out additional facts about the real-world industry. That is not required until you reach the T4 TOPCIMA case study.

A full revision of the technical theory behind the information in the Pre-seen.

The firm is fictitious. The issues facing the firm and its industry are written into the Pre-seen as examples of the application of technical subjects covered in the strategic syllabus. The Examiners may set requirements requiring you to explain this link and apply the theoretical techniques you have learned.

The Unseens on exam day will introduce new issues for you to deal with or comment on. So don't rely on coming to the exam day with a blueprint memorised for an answer based just on what you think about the Pre-seen.

Analysis of issues and problems presented in the Unseen material on exam day

Question 1 will provide a page or more of further information about the firm, but unlike the Pre-seen this will be tailored towards the particular syllabus of the paper. This will be followed by a series of requirements with mark allocations against them.

Your marks will be improved by:

1. *Judging the issue or opportunity in the context of the Pre-seen information in addition to the Unseen information.*

   For example: expanding a SWOT analysis to include factors from the Pre-seen; judging the investment project using Pre-seen information on present gearing levels or access to, and cost of, funds; identifying risks with reference also to control issues in the Pre-seen.

2. *Citing examples from the Pre-seen to support your discussion and judgements.*

   Use information from the Pre-seen case such as lessons from the history of the firm, financial analysis of performance, and assessments of the power of particular stakeholder groups.

   Including data from the Pre-seen in judgements on the suitability, acceptability and feasibility of options.

   Watch out for information in the Pre-seen case on stakeholder groups, missions, costs of capital, risk appetites and so on.

However experience has shown that the *majority* of the information that you are required to use will be in the Unseen material on exam day. The Pre-seen material is mainly additional background.

Illustration of benefits and implications of the recommendations you make

In the exams you may be required to make recommendations on an investment, evaluate the approach taken to strategy formulation, suggest new lines of business, or recommend improvements to control systems.

Your marks will be improved by:

1. *Including references to how your recommendation addresses issues in the Pre-seen as well as addressing the situation in the Unseen.*

    In a past exam the Pre-seen said that the firm has investors who had grumbled about the poor share price performance of the business. In the exams projects and forecasts had to be evaluated. A comment that your recommendations might raise the share price would have gained marks.

2. *Showing an appreciation that the Pre-seen material provides a framework for the detail in the Unseen and the requirements.*

    The Pre-seen will identify the industry and the mission of the organisation, its size, the amount of capital the firm has, and perhaps its dividend policy. You should ensure that how you evaluate issues, and the recommendations you make, are realistic. For example suggesting a huge investment programme for a small business with poor cash flows is likely to look ridiculous and attract few marks.

3. *Recognising the constraints on the firm imposed in the Pre-seen before recommending something inappropriate.*

    The Pre-seen may say that the market is mature, and that the firm has debt covenants that it cannot exceed. A student who recommended a huge investment into the industry would not get many marks.

Commentary on Pre-seen case study

IMPORTANT

Between now and the exam you have the opportunity to research the industry in which V – Travel Business operates. However **DO NOT** spend more than a few hours of your revision time on researching the Pre-seen case study. CIMA has stated that students should **not spend excessive time** on research. Your priority should be **lots of question practice**. As well as practising Section A questions, you should do plenty of the Section B questions included in your Practice and Revision Kits for each paper. Remember, Section B is also worth 50% of the marks for each exam.

Page 2

V is a private company, which means it does not presently suffer from pressure from financial markets and institutional investors. In the year to June 2012, it made SK$250m revenue and SK$35m net operating profit (page 6). It could be considering a flotation. This would subject it to new stakeholders, the need to conform to codes of corporate governance, and it would be required to focus on maximising shareholder wealth.

History of the company

V is not a real-world firm and it is unlikely to be closely based on one. But like many real-world travel companies, and retailers in general, V is facing the challenge of adapting a traditional store-based business to conducting business online.

From an E3 perspective, its traditional differentiating factor, customer service from branches, is losing relevance. According to Porter, loss of differentiation leads to loss of profitability as V becomes 'stuck in the middle', or at least it suffers falling margins as its differentiating factor of customer service ceases to be so relevant. A value chain analysis might be useful to assess which activities really do add value for V. Porter's 5 forces model can be used to analyse its situation as working in an industry where profits are being cut by the effect of a substitute, online selling, taking sales away. This is also subjecting firms to greater buyer power because pricing transparency and easy search facilities allow holiday-makers to shop around for bargains. It also permits market entry and disintermediation by rivals who no longer need to invest in branches.

Also, from an E3 perspective, the pre-seen states that V has been engaged in long-term planning for only 5 years, ie since 2007. This was to get loans of at least SK$15m to fund the investment in IT which V needed to establish its online business. Page 6 mentions loans of 30% of SK$50m repayable in June 2014 which suggests a 7 year loan taken out in June 2007. There may be a question involving the suitability of long-term planning for V in such a turbulent market. Perhaps it should adopt strategic management (or emergent strategy) approaches. However if it was to become a quoted company it would need to present reliable long-term financial forecasts to external investors.

From a P3 perspective the reliance on the IT system for 60% of its business subjects it to risk from breakdown, hacking, and online fraud. Be prepared to discuss the need for security controls, business continuity plans and so on. Also the Operations Director's comments on page 6 about lack of resources suggest wider issues with Information Strategy that P3 may also address.

Current structure of V's business

Note that the heading says 'current structure'. This is probably an indication that some questions in the exams will involve changes to its business portfolio and/or its relationship with other travel companies.

V follows a similar business model to real-world Swiss firm Kuoni.

www.kuoni.com/en/

Kuoni does not operate resorts or airlines. It 'crafts' holidays and 'hand picks' resorts and airlines. It operates 'stores' to enable tourists to enjoy personal consultations with its travel experts. It also has an online presence.

Kuoni is a more differentiated provider than V. V offers 'relatively cheap' adventure holidays, and self-catering family holidays. Kuoni has the same three groups of products: package, adventure, and prestige holidays and travel. It also has sport holidays, 'body and soul' holidays, special resort holidays, and a premium personal and corporate travel service. These could be future directions for V to take.

V does not act as an agent for other travel companies. This means it doesn't carry their brochures in its branches. E3 or P3 may ask students to analyse the possibility of V acting as an agent.

The pre-seen does not make clear whether V's holidays are sold by other agents as Kuoni's are. However, page 6 shows that V had SK\$70m of receivables on 30th June 2012, 28% of its annual earnings (SK\$70m/SK\$250m), which may in part be money owing from agents selling its holidays.

From a P3 perspective if the exam day material reveals that V does sell through agents, or is considering doing so, then there is risk to be considered. In 2011, some 41 UK tours operators and travel agents went bankrupt. Whilst their customers may have had their money refunded from industry schemes such as ATOL, these schemes would not ensure that a firm like V was paid the money it is owed for holidays the agents had sold.

Another P3 perspective is the management of risk to its destinations staff and its customers. Some Adventure holidays will have intrinsic risk, such as safaris, canoeing and white water rafting. Backpacking destinations are sometimes glamorous and risky in equal measure. But these risks are increased if V was to use the services of poor activities providers or bad accommodation. Various locations can impose risk from unsafe hotels, natural hazards, disease, terrorism or civil unrest. Be prepared to advise V on ways to mitigate these risks.

Many travel operators suffer from the risks of high operational gearing, a high ratio of fixed cost to total costs. If customer volumes and revenues fall they must still maintain the same service and so the same costs. Thus profits will fall sharply following relatively small reductions in customer numbers. V operates 50 branches in SK, and employs its own customer representatives at its destinations. If only a few holidays are sold at a destination the customer representative must still be there. If more holidays are booked on-line V still has to pay the costs of maintaining its branch network.

From an E3 perspective, V seems to have a muddled competitive strategy. With no strategic objectives it cannot judge the suitability of any strategic options. It has a differentiation focus position with Prestige holidays. It has a cost focus position with Adventure holidays. But Package holidays seem to be stuck in the middle, ranging from all-inclusive holidays to self catering. There may be questions around whether to close the branch network, whether to focus on particular resorts, whether to confine itself to offering particular sorts of holidays. Perhaps you may be asked to advise it on whether to add additional sorts of holidays such as sport holidays, cultural tours, or spa holidays, There will be the need for competitor analysis and other environmental analysis, and there would be change management issues too.

Support products

Insurance and foreign currency exchange are offered by real-world travel firms too as a valuable service to customers that generates additional income.

From a P3 perspective V will need to operate controls over these activities. The UK's Royal Society for the Prevention of Accidents (ROSPA) has called on travel firms to hire cars from reputable firms. This followed the death of a family when their poorly maintained hire car plunged off the side of a Spanish mountain road. The selling of some of these products may be regulated and require that staff be suitably qualified and that they follow strict procedures to ensure the customer is clear on what they are paying for. The handling of cash increases risk from theft, and forgery. Concerns have been expressed that the pre-paid currency cards could be used for money laundering and for this reason firms like V are required to conduct detailed background searches on applicants.

Page 3

Marketing of products

Note that its marketing literature provides the 'vast majority' of its business. The remaining minority of its business seems to be discount sales and it may suggest that V also makes use of aggregator sites such as lastminute.com to discount unsold holidays.

The impression is given that the package holidays are sometimes sold on price. This underlines the possibility that this type of holiday is where V suffers the strongest competition and makes poorest returns.

The costs of hard copy literature will be the costs of the colour brochures offered by holiday firms. These are expensive to produce, especially for a smaller operator like V that will not gain economies of scale from greater volumes of brochures and, presumably, produces three brochures to correspond to its three types of holiday product. From an E3 perspective these costs could be reduced if V sold some or all of its holidays without brochures, perhaps requiring it to embrace e-marketing and social media.

Sales structure

From a P3 perspective this section seems to include issues of control and risk.

Note that V is highly reliant on its IT systems for managing bookings from its two routes to market, online and branch. The P3 exam may give you more specific detail about aspects of, and problems with, the IT systems.

The discretion given to managers to offer discounts to match online prices does subject V to the risk that a manager may offer discounts without a valid reason. Also managers will need to strike a balance in order to maximise revenue. Some managers may be too conservative in offering discounts and lose customers as a result.

From an E3 perspective, the two sales channels seem to cannibalise sales and to duplicate costs. The 'clicks and mortar' strategy of having branches and online sales is common in many retail industries. It always raises the problem that prices often have to be lower in order to compete in the online market where pricing transparency is greater and the costs to the customer of comparing and searching out a bargain are much lower. Shops can try to charge more because they give advice and so on, as well as to cover the higher operating costs of a ground-based operation.

V could consider focusing its shops on selling Adventure and Prestige holidays, where advice and personal service may be of greater value to customers, and to migrate its Package holidays exclusively to the online sales channel.

But without more detailed information on the costs and revenues of V, broken down by type of holiday, this is just conjecture.

Financial information

This section seems to take us towards the issues of segment profitability. We are told the revenues from each type of holiday but there is only an overall profit ratio given, 10%.

This overall profit ratio is not very helpful. It is derived from the post tax profit (page 6: SK$24/SK$250 = 9.6%) and therefore contains finance income and finance costs that are independent of sales revenue and are not influenced by the types of holiday sold. A more useful ratio would be the operating profit to sales ratio of 14% (page 6: SK$35/SK$250).

Calculating the profit from each type of holiday would be complex for V. There are shared overheads because they are sold by the same staff from the same shops. There are also associated sales to include from the Support products.

P3 may ask you to comment on one or more new management accounting measures that may help management assess the business better. These may include measures of product or branch success, and may require assessment of qualitative as well as quantitative issues. Note that at present management are happy to pay bonuses based on sales on the grounds that sales appear to be a function of V's 99% quality rating. What would happen if the quality rating was not robust and some customers were dissatisfied?

From an F3 perspective, the seasonal cash flows require careful management.

Financial objectives

Increasing earnings whilst maintaining dividend can be conflicting objectives because growing a business often needs retained profits to finance the required investment. Page 2 gives an example of this income-growth trade off where it states that V needed external funding (ie had to borrow debt as there are no external shareholders) to pay for its new IT and IS investment 5 years ago.

This data on earnings growth and dividend payout may be included for several purposes:

For F3 these would be relevant data for a share valuation exercise. Page 5 of this pre-seen tells us that a major shareholder wants to exit and that the Board is considering attracting new equity investment.

For E3 these are potential constraints. A strategic investment will need to demonstrate 'acceptability' against these.

Page 6 details a further constraint that may affect investment. This is the debt covenant that requires that V's capital gearing does not exceed 50%.

Foreign exchange risk

This section is of potential relevance to the P3 exam. It details foreign exchange risk and risk from volatility of aircraft fuel prices. Be prepared to evaluate the methods V could employ to manage these risks. For example, currency options

on the currency of the destinations and the home currencies of the airlines. Appropriate legal wording on aircraft fuel surcharges in customer agreements would transfer risk. However these are not popular with families and they caused a backlash when two UK operators introduced them in March 2011, not least because there are few, if any, cases of travel companies refunding fares to customers when the price of fuel falls below the level expected.

Page 4

Board composition and operational responsibilities

Four key points stand out from this section:

1. The Board does not conform to the best practices of corporate governance (note V is not a UK company and neither is it listed so the UK Corporate Governance Code does not apply to it, although you can use the UK Code as a helpful benchmark). The Chairman is also the CEO and the Board has no non-executive directors.

2. There is likely to be a succession issue because the Executive Chairman has no-one in his family he would wish to help run V.

3. There is no Marketing Director despite V being a retail business.

4. Who is actually responsible for the operation of the online business? The primary focus of the Operations Director seems to be on the high street branches and managing the 50 store managers. Is the Operations Director also in charge of the online operations or has the IT Director taken charge of this?

These are principally relevant from a P3 perspective because they indicate potentially poor strategic control over V.

They would also be relevant from the perspectives of E3 if, in the exams, the additional unseen material required you to discuss some aspects of V admitting new equity and/or heading towards becoming quoted. This could be a scenario where V is considering a full listing (unlikely given its size, although there may be opportunities in a smaller, AIM-type, market) or perhaps where a venture capitalist is considering investing and you are discussing potential exit routes in 5 years via a listing. You would need to point out that listing requirements would require a better-balanced Board. In E3 you might be asked to advise on the sorts of changes to which such a step might lead.

In the exams you can expect to be required to assume the role of the part-qualified management accountant reporting to the Finance Director. As such, you would be bound by CIMA's Ethical Code. You should expect questions involving this.

Shareholding

This is basic information that shows the Executive Chairman's holding is significant. He also anticipates a dividend of SK$9.98m from the 2012 profits of V (SK$24m x 80% x 52%) which he assumes will grow at 5% a year. No cost of equity is given in the pre-seen and it cannot be calculated. But if we assume a 10% cost of equity this would suggest the Executive Chairman's 46.8m shares (52% of 90m shares) are worth SK$ 210m (SK$9.98 x 1.05/0.10-0.05). Put another way, V's shares are worth about SK$4.48 each using the dividend growth model of valuation and assuming a 10% cost of equity.

In the F3 examination you might be expected to calculate the cost of equity for V by using data from a listed travel company and adjusting it for gearing. You should also remember that as an unlisted company V's shares would be discounted because they are illiquid. Each of the remaining directors would also need to suffer a further discount because each holds a minority interest.

Employees

Two features stand out from this section:

1. From a P3 perspective there seems to be risk of poor compliance, poor advice and mis-selling. The staff are not formally trained in the products they sell or the procedures they should follow when they start with the company. The preseen does not make clear what the updates about products are. If they are just newsletters rather than formal training sessions, staff may not bother to read them properly or misunderstand guidance in them. These staff advise on the suitability of holidays for the customer, deal in foreign exchange and pre-loaded charge cards, and sell insurance. There is significant reputation risk to V here from the consequences of poor advice. One UK travel firm was successfully sued by the next of kin of a couple who had hired a car in the USA but the travel firm

had not warned them of the dangers of driving the car with the windows down in the crime-ridden area around the car pick up lot. The scandal over mis-selling of Payment Protection Insurance in the UK was due to staff being paid bonuses to sell these policies as an add on to selling loans and mortgages. V's bonus scheme seems likely to lead to similar dysfunctional and perhaps unethical selling to customers, possibly customers deliberately being sold unsuitable products or being told wrongly that they are obliged to take out travel insurance with V.

2. From an E3 perspective these are the staff that would be subject to change management. In the exam it is important to bear in mind this information to ensure any advice you give is practical. There is little natural wastage of staff, which would make downsizing impossible without compulsory redundancies. They are spread across corporate centre, 50 shops, and a large number of destinations.

Safety

From a P3 perspective, this paragraph seems to underline earlier analysis of the need for V to ensure the selected car hire, hotels, and transfers are safe. This requires proper risk assessment procedures.

The reference to illness on holiday also reminds us that V should have contingency plans in place to deal with sudden problems such as outbreaks of illness from food poisoning in a particular hotel or, as has happened, ear and skin infections from swimming pools and spas.

From an E3 perspective, there are issues of CSR and ethics to consider. If V believes there is a problem at a resort it needs to decide how to respond to it. Also there is a balance to be struck between allowing customers on adventure holidays to assess risks for themselves and deciding to stop selling a particular sort of holiday.

Executive Chairman's statement to the press

This statement was made 7 months before the end of V's financial year. The results on page 6 have three limitations:

- There are no prior years to compare them with to assess trends and growth

- There is no data on comparable travel firms to assess V's margins and profitability against

- They are historic. The seasonal nature of holidays means that by January 2012 the Executive Chairman would be reporting mainly on the 2011 summer season, and would not have a clear view of the prospects for summer 2012.

This means that this paragraph, and the final accounts on page 6, may not be a reliable guide to the financial condition of V in November 2012, the date of the first exam sittings based on this pre-seen material.

Note that the Executive Chairman states an intention to 'expand and diversify' V's holiday product range. This has potential impact on all three Strategic exams.

From an E3 perspective, diversification means new products and markets. The examiner may ask you to evaluate new sorts of holidays, or new destinations. This would need to take into account suitability, acceptability and feasibility. It might also include environmental assessment of new countries. One big issue in the travel industry is 'sustainable tourism'. Sustainability was examined in E3 in relation to supermarkets in May 2012, so the examiner may expect you to discuss this in relation to travel in the November 2012 or March 2013 exams.

From a P3 perspective, expansion and diversification imply greater risk and a weakening of controls. New holidays will impose new risks on V and will require proper risk assessments and development of new controls. There will be new risks, including legal and currency risks, attached to operating in new countries.

From an F3 perspective, expansion and diversification may require additional funding and, through changing risk profile, may also affect V's cost of capital.

Board meeting

This meeting gives voice to the concerns that have been discussed in this analysis. There seem to be three topics mentioned, one for each examination:

E3: Customer relationship marketing. Be prepared to explain this term, ie it values retaining customers and maximising their spend over time rather than focusing on unit sales as transactions marketing does. You must also be able to explain the techniques that may support it, such as using IS to deliver customer relationship management solutions, and the importance of assessing lifecycle customer profitability. Note that the Executive Chairman does not seem to understand this concept. Note also the reference to product profitability. Expect a question requiring you to explain the difference between customer profitability and product profitability and setting you computations on one or both of these.

P3: IT/IS project implementation and risks. Potentially this may involve V in outsourcing its IT/IS provision. P3 could look at any aspect of information strategy – strategic data needs of the business (IS) , facilities available (IT), ways information is made available (IM).

F3: advising on ways to raise finance.

Page 5

Retirement of the Executive Chairman

This small paragraph introduces several potential questions, mainly of relevance to the F3 examination

- Valuation of the shares of V

- Considerations in introducing new shareholders, in particular venture capitalists

- Capital restructuring and alternative methods of financing V. In this connection note that page 6 shows that V has SK$123m of non-current assets and only SK$50m of loans, and its capital gearing stands at 40% (SK$50m/ SK$50m+SK$75mn) and therefore it can raise a further SK$25m of debt without breaching its maximum debt covenant of 50% (ie loans SK$75m = EquitySK$75m).

IMPORTANT

In the analysis above we have discussed how certain topics introduced in the Pre-seen could be developed in the Unseen scenarios for each paper. However, that does **NOT** mean you can question spot. The Unseens could include topics that are not mentioned at all in the Pre-seen, so don't be surprised to see new issues being included in any of the exams.

BPP
LEARNING MEDIA

Tackling Question 1

You should aim to spend at least half of your 20 minutes reading time on each strategic paper reading the new Unseen information you are given about V – Travel Business in Question 1 and the question requirements. You should highlight and annotate the key points on the question paper.

You'll improve your chances of success by following a step-by-step approach to the questions along the following lines.

 Read the opening paragraph to set the scene

Look out in particular for changes from the Pre-seen that the opening paragraph highlights, or factors influencing the business decisions you may be discussing in your answer (business strategies, financial resources and control systems).

 Read the requirements

You need to identify the knowledge areas being tested and what information will therefore be significant.

 Identify the action verbs

These convey the level of skill you need to exhibit. See the list of verbs at the start of the answer bank. Make sure you have highlighted **all** the verbs in the question. Often question parts have more than one verb, and students fail by taking no notice of the second verb.

 Identify what each part of the question requires

When planning, you will need to make sure that you aren't reproducing the same material in more than one part of the question.

Don't worry if the research you've done on the Pre-seen material doesn't appear to be relevant to any of the question requirements. You should expect the Unseen to include the material that you need to use to score lots of the marks.

 Check the mark allocation to each part

This shows you the depth and number of points anticipated and helps allocate time.

 Read the scenario carefully

You need to highlight significant new information that the Unseen provides, as this will provide the focus for your answer.

- New data may give you a fresh perspective compared with the Pre-seen
- The Unseen may build on hints given in the Pre-seen
- The Unseen may give information about changes in situations described in the Pre-seen

For P3 look out for risks and weaknesses, also procedures, systems and controls that are currently in place. Any risks that have been highlighted are likely to be very relevant to your answer. Terms such as exposure, uncertainty and probability are likely to highlight key risks.

For E3 consider significant changes in the business's environment, particularly new or increased opportunities or threats. Make sure you appreciate the importance of any new strategic options that have emerged. If V – Travel Business has to undergo major changes, and the question asks about change management, you'll need to watch for the factors that may affect the success or otherwise of change management. You may also have to discuss how to measure the success of a change management strategy.

For F3 there will be most probably be significant new financial data, giving more information about content covered in the Pre-seen, information about future results, or a new project or investment. You'll need to consider indications of uncertainty in the data that you're given, highlighting words such as variance or volatility. You'll need to analyse major new data carefully, but **don't neglect** the written parts of the Unseen. These may contain important new information, for example alterations in financial objectives or changes in the financing constraints that V faces.

Put points under headings related to requirements (eg by margin notes). Consider the techniques you'll need to use.

Consider the consequences of the points you've identified

Remember that in the answer you will often have to provide recommendations based on the information you've been given. Consider the limitations of any analysis you undertake or other factors that may impact upon your recommendations.

Also think how significant the points you identify are. Not everything you highlight will be vital to answering the question, and you may need to prioritise the points if you are under time pressure.

Write a plan

You may be able to do this on the question paper as often there will be at least one blank page in the question booklet.

You must ensure when planning your answer that you use the Unseen information appropriately. You can bring in the Pre-seen information as well if it's relevant. You should include the results of any research you've done in your answer **ONLY IF RELEVANT**. **DO NOT BRAIN DUMP** all your research into your answer, no matter what the question requirements are. You will receive **NO MARKS** for irrelevant material, however much time you've spent researching it. You must answer the **QUESTION SET** and not the question you hoped would be set.

Check quickly before you start writing that your plan covers all necessary points, excludes irrelevant material and is well-structured. Assess also how much detail you will include. To demonstrate good application skills, you'll need to explain the relevance and significance of the points you're making, but you'll also have to remember the time constraints. Confirm that there is no duplication between answers to different question parts.

Write the answer

Make every effort to present your answer clearly. Paragraphs should have headers that relate to the question requirements or key information in the scenario. Underline key numbers and show your workings clearly. Also remember that the Unseen information, though important, should be used to **support your answer** where appropriate. You should avoid just copying out chunks of the Unseen.

You may find that the preparation you've done has helped, and you have a lot of material that you can use in your answer to Question 1. However, remember also that the Section B questions in each paper are also worth together 50% of the marks. You must avoid spending so long on Question 1 that you throw away mark-scoring opportunities because you do not have enough time to answer fully two questions from Section B.

PRE-SEEN CASE STUDY

Pre-seen case study for Strategic level examinations – Papers E3, P3 and F3

For examinations in November 2012 and March 2013

PRE-SEEN MATERIAL, PROVIDED IN ADVANCE FOR PREPARATION AND STUDY FOR THE EXAMINATIONS IN NOVEMBER 2012 AND MARCH 2013.
INSTRUCTIONS FOR POTENTIAL CANDIDATES
This booklet contains the pre-seen material for the above examinations. It will provide you with the contextual information that will help you prepare yourself for the examinations.
You may not take this copy of the pre-seen material into the examination hall. A fresh copy will be provided on each of the examination days as part of the examination paper.
Section A of each of the three Strategic level papers (E3, P3 and F3) will be based on this material.
Unseen material will be provided on the examination day; this will comprise further context and the examination question requirements (a maximum of four compulsory questions, totalling 50 marks).
You will not be expected to have any knowledge of any other examination questions or unseen materials based on this pre-seen case study.
Section B of each of the three Strategic level papers (E3, P3 and F3) will NOT be based on this material.
The examination will last for three hours. You will be allowed 20 minutes reading time **before the examination begins** during which you should read the question paper and, if you wish, make annotations on the question paper. However, you will **not** be allowed, **under any circumstances**, to either begin writing or to use your calculator during the reading time.

Pre-seen case study

V, a private limited company in a European country (SK), which is outside the Eurozone, was founded in 1972. The currency in SK is SK$. V is a travel business that offers three holiday (vacation) products. It has a network of 50 branches in a number of major cities throughout SK.

History of the company
V achieved steady growth until six years ago, when it found that its market share was eroding due to customers increasingly making online bookings with its competitors. Direct bookings for holidays through the internet have increased dramatically in recent years. Many holidaymakers find the speed and convenience of booking flights, accommodation or complete holidays online outweighs the benefits of discussing holiday alternatives with staff in a branch.

V's board had always taken the view that the friendly direct personal service that V offers through its branch network is a major differentiating factor between itself and other travel businesses and that this is highly valued by its customers. However, V found that in order to continue to compete it needed to establish its own online travel booking service, which it did five years ago. Until this point, V's board had never engaged in long-term planning. It had largely financed growth by reinvestment of funds generated by the business. The large investment in IT and IS five years ago required significant external funding and detailed investment appraisal.

Much of V's business is now transacted online through its website to the extent that 60% of its revenue in the year ended 30 June 2012 was earned through online bookings.

Current structure of V's business
V offers three types of holiday product. These are known within V as Package, Adventure and Prestige Travel. V only sells its own products and does not act as an agent for any other travel companies. It uses the services of other companies engaged in the travel industry such as chartered airlines and hotels which it pays for directly on behalf of its customers.

Package
"Package" provides holidays mainly for families with children aged up to their late teens. These typically are for accommodation in hotels (where meals are part of the package) or self-catering apartments (where no meals are provided within the package).

Adventure
"Adventure" caters for people aged mainly between 20 and 30, who want relatively cheap adventure based holidays such as trekking, sailing and cycling or who wish to go on inexpensive back-packing holidays mainly in Europe and Asia.

Prestige Travel
"Prestige Travel" provides expensive and bespoke holidays mainly sold to couples whose children have grown up and left home. The Prestige Travel product only provides accommodation in upmarket international hotel chains in countries across the world.

All three of these products provide holidays which include flights to and from the holiday destinations and hotel or self-catering accommodation. V has its own customer representatives available at the holiday destinations to provide support to its customers. All-inclusive holidays (in which all food and drinks are provided within the holiday price) are offered within each of the three product offerings.

Support products
V supports its main products by offering travel insurance and foreign currency exchange. The travel insurance, which is provided by a major insurance company and for which V acts as an agent, is usually sold along with the holidays both by branch staff and by staff dealing with online bookings.

Currency exchange is available to anyone through V's branches irrespective of whether or not the customer has bought a holiday product from V. A new currency exchange product is provided by V through which a customer purchases an amount of currency, either in SK's home

currency (SK$) or else in a foreign currency and this is credited on to a plastic card. The card is then capable of being read by automated teller machines (ATM's) in many countries across the world allowing the customer to withdraw cash in the local currency up to the amount that has been credited on to the card.

Marketing of products
V relies for the vast majority of its business on the literature, available in hard copy and online, which it provides on the holiday products it sells. Exceptionally, V is able to offer some of its existing holiday products at discount prices. These may be offered under any of the three main products offered but they are mostly cut-price holiday deals which are available under the Package holiday product label.

Sales structure
Staff in each of the 50 branches accept bookings from customers and all branches have direct IT access to head office. Online enquiries and bookings are received and processed centrally at head office, which is located in SK's capital city.

Branch managers have some discretion to offer discounts on holidays to customers. V offers a discount to customers who buy holidays through its online bookings. The branch managers have authority to reduce the price of a holiday booked at the branch up to the amount of the online discount if they feel it is necessary to do so in order to make the sale.

Financial information
V's revenue, split across the holiday and support products offered, for the financial year ended 30 June 2012 is summarised as follows:

	Revenue SK$ million
Package	90
Adventure	60
Prestige Travel	95
Support products	5

The overall net operating profit generated in the financial year to 30 June 2012 was SK$35 million and the profit for the year was SK$24 million, giving a profit to sales ratio of just under 10%. V's cash receipts fluctuate because of seasonal variations and also because V's customers pay for their holidays shortly before they depart.

Further details, including extracts from V's income statement for the year ended 30 June 2012 and statement of financial position as at 30 June 2012 are shown in Appendix 1.

Financial objectives
V's key financial objectives are as follows:

1. To grow earnings by, on average, 5% a year.
2. To pay out 80% of profits as dividends.

Foreign exchange risk
V has high exposure to foreign exchange risk as its revenues received and payments made are frequently in different currencies. It normally settles hotel bills and support costs, such as transfers between hotels and airports in the local currencies of the countries where the hotels are located. It normally pays charter airlines in the airline's home currency. Scheduled airline charges are settled in the currency required by the particular airline.

V is exposed to fluctuations in the cost of aircraft fuel incurred by airlines which are passed on to travel businesses. It has often been necessary for V to require its customers to make a supplementary payment to cover the cost of increases in aircraft fuel, sometimes after the customer had thought that the final payment for the holiday had been made.

Board composition and operational responsibilities

The Board of Directors comprises five people: an Executive Chairman (who also fulfils the role of Chief Executive), a Finance Director, an Operations Director, an IT Director and a Human Resources Director. The Executive Chairman founded the business in 1972. He has three grown-up children, two of whom successfully pursue different business interests and are not engaged in V's business at all. The third child, a son, is currently taking a "year out" from study and is going to university next year to study medicine.

The branch managers all report directly to the Operations Director. In addition, the Operations Director is responsible for liaising with airlines and hotels which provide the services offered by V's promotional literature. The IT Director is responsible for V's website and online enquiries and bookings. The Finance Director is responsible for V's financial and management accounting systems and has a small team of accountancy staff, including a part-qualified management accountant, reporting to her. The Human Resources Director has a small team of staff reporting to him.

Shareholding

There are 90 million SK$0.10 (10 cent) shares in issue and the shareholdings are as follows:

	% holding
Executive Chairman	52
Finance Director	12
Operations Director	12
IT Director	12
Human Resources Director	12

Employees

V employs 550 full-time equivalent staff. Turnover of staff is relatively low. High performance rewards in terms of bonuses are paid to staff in each branch if it meets or exceeds its quarterly sales targets. Similarly, staff who deal with online bookings receive a bonus if the online bookings meet or exceed quarterly sales targets. V's staff, both in the branches and those employed in dealing with online bookings, also receive an additional bonus if they are able to sell travel insurance along with a holiday product to customers.

Employee development for staff who are in direct contact with the public is provided through updates on products which V offers. Each member of branch and online booking staff undertakes a two day induction programme at the commencement of their employment with V. The emphasis of the induction programme is on customer service not on details relating to the products as it is expected that new staff will become familiar with such product details as they gain experience within V.

Safety

V publicly states that it takes great care to ensure that its customers are as safe as possible while on holiday. To date, V has found that accidents while on holiday are mainly suffered by very young children, Adventure customers and elderly customers. There has been an increase in instances over the last year where customers in resort hotels have suffered severe stomach complaints. This has particularly been the case in hotels located in resorts in warm climates.

Executive Chairman's statement to the press

V's Executive Chairman was quoted in the national press in SK in January 2012 as saying, "We are maintaining a comparatively high level of revenues and operating profit. This is in a period when our competitors are experiencing very difficult trading conditions. We feel we are achieving this due to our particular attention to customer service. He cited V's 40 years of experience in the travel industry and a previous 99% satisfaction rating from its customers as the reasons for its success. He went on to state that V intends to expand and diversify its holiday product range to provide more choice to customers.

Board meeting

At the next board meeting which took place after the Executive Chairman's statement to the press, the Operations Director expressed some concern. He cast doubt on whether V was able

to provide sufficient funding, marketing and IT/IS resources to enable the product expansion to which the Executive Chairman referred. The Operations Director was of the opinion that V places insufficient emphasis on customer relationship marketing. The Finance Director added at the same meeting that while V presently remained profitable overall, some products may be more profitable than others.

The Executive Chairman responded by saying that V's high level of customer service provides a sufficiently strong level of sales without the need to incur any other marketing costs. He added that since V achieved a high profit to sales ratio, which it has managed to maintain for a number of years, it really didn't matter about the profits generated by each customer group.

Retirement of the Executive Chairman

The Executive Chairman formally announced to the Board in July 2012 that he intends to retire on 30 June 2013 and wishes to sell part of his shareholding in the company. The Board members believe the time is now right for V, given its expansion plans, to enter a new stage in its financing arrangements, in the form of either debt or equity from new providers.

Extracts from V's income statement and statement of financial position

Income statement for the year ended 30 June 2012

	Notes	SK$ million
Revenue		250
Operating costs		(215)
Net operating profit		35
Interest income		3
Finance costs		(4)
Corporate income tax	1	(10)
PROFIT FOR THE YEAR		24

Statement of financial position as at 30 June 2012

	Notes	SK$ million
ASSETS		
Non-current assets		123
Current assets		
Inventories		3
Trade and other receivables		70
Cash and cash equivalents		37
Total current assets		110
Total assets		233
EQUITY AND LIABILITIES		
Equity		
Share capital	2	9
Share premium		6
Retained earnings		60
Total equity		75
Non-current liabilities		
Long-term borrowings	3	50
Revenue received in advance		3
Current liabilities		
Trade and other payables		35
Revenue received in advance		70
Total liabilities		158
Total equity and liabilities		233

Notes:

1. The corporate income tax rate can be assumed to be 30%.
2. There are 90 million SK$0.10 (10 cent) shares currently in issue.
3. 30% of the long-term borrowings are due for repayment on 30 June 2014. The remainder is due for re-payment on 30 June 2020. There are debt covenants in operation currently which restrict V from having a gearing ratio measured by long-term debt divided by long-term debt plus equity of more than 50%.

End of Pre-seen Material

QUESTIONS

Question 1

Unseen case material

A mission statement for V

Following his statement in the national press, the Executive Chairman is keen to implement a new strategy prior to his retirement and has appealed to his fellow directors to put forward appropriate proposals.

It quickly transpired that the other directors had been researching their own strategies for some time so there was no shortage of ideas. However, with a diverse range of proposals on the table, there was no consensus as to which would be the most successful.

In order to resolve the deadlock, the Finance Director proposed that a mission statement for V was prepared. The Executive Chairman immediately advised that his recent comment to the national media would be adopted as V's mission statement and used as a basis for selecting new strategies:

> "V intends to expand and diversify its holiday product range to provide more choice to customers."

However, even with the new mission statement, the directors were unable to agree a clear plan of action. The Finance Director proposed setting objectives, at which point the Executive Chairman lost his patience, saying: "I want people who are going to deliver results. All you are delivering is waffle."

The Finance Director tried to explain the concept of mission statements and objectives, but met with resistance from the other directors who agreed with the Executive Chairman. She therefore asked for a formal opportunity to explain why she felt these matters needed to be addressed. With great reluctance from the other directors, this has been added to the agenda for the next meeting.

New IT system

One thing that all the directors agree with is the need for better IT. V does have a website which generates 60% of its revenue but, having been built five years ago as part of the last IT upgrade, it is now showing its age. A recent online customer survey showed that customers were unimpressed with the website, with several describing it as "quite boring." V does not use any social media to help with its marketing.

Furthermore, V's internal IT systems are limited. When a customer books a holiday online, a member of V's staff prints out a copy of the booking and keys it into V's booking system. At the end of each day, a report is produced and emailed to the various providers. These providers check availability and confirm the booking with V the following day. However, with the prices fluctuating (sometimes hourly), V occasionally finds that the price has changed since it contractually agreed to the customer's booking. Any gain or loss on this is absorbed by V as part of its margin. On some occasions, the holiday is no longer available, in which case V has to contact the customer and offer alternatives. It is estimated that, for every SK$100 of online revenue received, a further 30 cents of revenue is lost due to V not being able to honour the booking and the customer going elsewhere.

The IT director has proposed that V invests in a new booking system. This software package would automate the existing process, minimising the need for human input. Although there would be no visible change to the website pages, when a customer made an online booking on V's website, the booking would be automatically forwarded to the relevant supplier. This would ensure that any alterations to availability or price would be incorporated into the offer to the customer before the order is confirmed. The IT Director is convinced that this will help to recover the margin on lost sales. It is also expected to prove a hit with suppliers, who are finding V's methods of communication increasingly archaic and frustrating to administer.

One of the benefits of adopting such a system, the IT director went on to explain, is that separate systems will now be linked together, ensuring faster and more accurate sharing of internal data. So, for example, the system would provide all the data to the finance office to enable the preparation of monthly management accounts. The current process involves reports from the booking system being sent to the finance department monthly but, due to compatibility issues, the data has to be manually keyed. This uses a high volume of resource at an already hectic time of the month and has caused problems in the past when data entry errors were made.

Reactions to the IT proposal

The Finance Director is cautiously optimistic about the new booking system, having experienced the errors and frustrations of the existing process. However, she is becoming increasingly frustrated that her department cannot obtain any data about the breakdown of revenue and profit for each product area. At the last meeting, she made her feelings clear – "At this point, I don't care how you present the data as long as you give it to me!"

In the absence of a Marketing Director, there is a Marketing Manager who is co-opted onto the board on an ad hoc basis as required. He is very disappointed that the project does not incorporate any marketing initiatives. He is resisting the project on the grounds that it will not make any difference to the way he markets V's products and services. What he wants, instead, is major investment in a new website and e-marketing campaigns.

The Operations Director is also concerned about the project from an operational perspective. He has warned that previous attempts to automate the holiday booking process have failed and "caused more problems than they solved". He and his department argue that the manual processes are the only way of ensuring that accurate data is maintained and that, to do away with them risks "customers being sent to Timbuktu instead of Thailand".

The HR Director is concerned about the staffing implications of the new system and has warned that the associated costs (eg redundancies) may well outweigh the benefits.

Costing the system

Given the wariness of his fellow directors, the IT Director has prepared his own costings for the system. The supplier he has chosen, MNO, has a very good reputation for implementing systems like this, which meant that he felt no need to look any further. MNO has quoted SK$250,000 for the hardware upgrades that will be required to enable V to run the new system. The software licence is paid annually in advance at a charge of $3,000 per user. On top of that, training will be required for all registered users at an initial cost of SK$500 each. This training will be repeated in a "top up" format at the start of each subsequent year at a cost of $250 per registered user.

V currently employs 13 full-time staff who process the internet orders. The IT Director is confident that this figure can be reduced to 8. However, for the first three months, he plans to recruit three extra temporary staff to help smooth the transition from the old system to the new one. Given the highly routine nature of the work, the IT Director is confident that these staff will do exactly the same work (and receive exactly the same training) as their permanent colleagues and will therefore be paid the same salary of SK$20,000 (pro rata). At the end of three months, he plans to let the three temporary staff go and make five permanent positions redundant.

Looking back at the last IT investment, the IT Director notes that a cost of capital of 6% was used, which he intends to use for this project also. In the absence of any more accurate forecasts, he is assuming that revenue and margins will remain constant for the foreseeable future.

The requirement for this question is on the following page

Required

(a) In the context of V, **explain** to the board what constitutes an effective mission statement and **evaluate** the one adopted by V. **(12 marks)**

(b) **Recommend,** with reasons, four new objectives for V. Your answer should use an appropriate performance measurement framework to ensure that a full range of key business issues is addressed. **(8 marks)**

(c) (i) **Analyse** the concerns expressed by the directors and the Marketing manager about the proposed IT system, and **advise** the IT Director how these concerns could be addressed. **(8 marks)**

(ii) **Analyse** the possible concerns of TWO other stakeholders and **advise** the IT Director how these concerns could be addressed. **(4 marks)**

(d) **Evaluate** the financial information provided by the IT director and **advise** the board whether the IT system being proposed is suitable for V. **(18 marks)**

Note: There are 7 marks in available in part (d) for your calculations using the data given by the IT Director.

(Total marks for question = 50 marks)

BPP
LEARNING MEDIA

Question 2

V – Travel Business

Unseen case material

Changes to the board

Last month, the Executive Chairman was taken ill during a board meeting and had to be rushed to hospital. On the advice of his doctors, he has resigned as Executive Chairman with immediate effect, although he plans to retain his shares in the company. In a letter to the other members of the board, he explained: "While I have great pride in what I have achieved at V over the years, it has been at a considerable personal cost. This illness has been a wake-up call for me to spend more time with my family while I still can. I'll miss this company – after all I set it up myself forty years ago. However, I have every confidence in your collective ability to take V from strength to strength. Of course, I'm still the majority shareholder, so I'll be keeping a close eye on the business to make sure that you do this!"

With the agreement of the Operations Director (OD), IT Director (ITD) and HR Director (HRD), the Finance Director (FD) has assumed the role of Executive Chairman and Chief Executive.

Managing the product range

In spite of the outgoing Executive Chairman's positive statements about V's position, the reality is that both revenue and profit have been declining significantly year-on-year. Although this decline is not as dramatic as other similar travel businesses, the directors all agree that this position is not sustainable. However, this is where the agreement ends.

FD and IT are concerned about the current product range and believe the solution is to expand into new products and markets. OD and HR, on the other hand, see the current offering as integral to V's survival. In the words of OD, "If we can't get our core product range to work, what makes you think we could succeed with a new range that isn't underpinned by forty years of experience?" In an attempt to resolve the impasse, ITD prepared the following report and presented it at the board meeting.

REPORT

To: The board of directors

From: ITD

Date: 1 Nov 2012

Re.:   Changes to product range

Introduction

Our current product range is no longer working. Although the % profit margin is remaining constant, we have been seeing a worrying decline in revenue across all products. While our existing customers like us, this is not enough to maintain our market share and we are therefore losing out to our competitors. To make matters even worse, more and more customers are avoiding travel agents altogether and booking their holidays online direct with the provider, so we're fighting for a share of an ever-reducing market.

People used to like our product range but, forty years on, it's starting to feel stale. We would expect to see customers moving through our products as they mature (ie start with Adventure, move on to Package when they have children, and end up with Prestige when the children leave home) but this just isn't happening. Bearing in mind that all our products are marketed under a single "V" brand, this tells me that we just aren't offering the products our customers want.

The only way I can see of us recovering our market share is to offer more products under the same "V" brand. With this in mind, I have identified three possible initiatives:

Health Tourism

A number of our Prestige Travel customers are now over 70 years old – I suppose this is what comes of setting up a strong brand forty years ago! At this stage of life, many are no longer up to travelling long distances to visit the same exotic locations they used to. Furthermore, a significant number are in need of additional support with day-to-day living which, in the home, is either provided by family members or visiting "home helps". [A "home help" visits a housebound person up to three times daily to help with washing, dressing and other day-to-day domestic assistance.]

I'm sure you will already be aware of travel agencies that cater specifically for retired people. However, a new company called T has gone one stage further and has just started offering luxury hotel accommodation in SK specifically for guests and their families who rely on home help. There is excellent access for those with limited mobility, properly designed and equipped bedrooms and an appropriate level of care and support.

Holidays such as these therefore serve two purposes. As well as providing a holiday to those who might not otherwise have been able to go on one, they also give a break to family members who are normally the main carers. Although other places offer respite care for people in this situation, T is unique in that it offers a five star service. In fact, the facilities are so good, that it has also opened to retired people without any domestic or healthcare needs who simply want to enjoy its excellent location and facilities!

The combination of a world-class hotel and a high level of assistance means that this sort of holiday doesn't come cheap. T charges SK$2,500 per person per night all inclusive (ie all meals and drinks included), although this price includes access to all facilities including sauna and swimming pool, and an appropriate level of "home help" type support. V would receive 5% commission from each sale it arranged.

We would plan to sell this product in branches and online. T's marketing director has warned that this is a highly specialised product which requires careful training. Luckily, T offers a two day residential training course to ensure sales staff fully understand the complexities of the product. At $5,000 per person, this seemed very expensive but, as T's marketing director pointed out, the staff will be picking up valuable skills in assertive selling which will enable them to maximise sales, not just of T's hotel, but also of other V products. Based on his recommendation, I propose sending two people from each of our branches on this training.

Over a five year contract, T has advised us that we should expect to sell the following:

	Year 1	Year 2	Year 3	Year 4	Year 5
Number of customer nights per year	5,000	6,000	7,000	8,000	9,000

Some of these customers would have purchased other holidays from V. I estimate that 27½% of these customers would have spent the same amount of money on another V holiday, which would have generated us a net operating margin of 15%. The remaining 72½% of customers will be new to V.

I have noticed that T is still advertising for healthcare staff to work in the hotel. When I mentioned it to T's marketing director, he explained that they were experiencing a few recruitment problems. It surprised me that there was no reference to needing an appropriate healthcare qualification but, as the marketing director pointed out, most of the care work is "pretty basic stuff". Either way, he has guaranteed that there will be sufficient staff to look after all its guests.

Conferences

There is a serious shortage of high quality, large-scale conference venues in SK. In fact, A-Centre is the only properly-equipped venue in the country that can accommodate 5,000 delegates. Although the venue itself is first class, A-Centre does not organise catering, and instructs delegations to make its own arrangements (although food from outside caterers can be served on site). This is a source of frustration to many large organisations who want to pass on the hassle to someone else, but the absence of any suitable alternative venue gives A-Centre a captive market.

My proposal, therefore, is to block book the A-Centre for 30 days at SK$30,000 per day and then re-sell them to organisations as part of a fully serviced conference. We wouldn't make much of a margin on the actual venue (although, if an organisation was desperate for dates we had, we could obviously slam the price right up), but we could sub-contract the catering and charge a 15% mark-up for the client. I have a specific caterer in mind, who is a good friend of mine. After a serious personal crisis, he has just started out in the catering industry and is desperate to make a go of it. I've known him for many years and can vouch for his integrity. Nobody else seems to want to work with him and a contract like ours will give him just the break he needs and deserves.

	Worst outcome	Most likely outcome	Best outcome
Probability	35%	50%	15%
Number of bookings (each for 1 day)	15	20	30
Average revenue from venue hire (per day)	$35,000	$29,000	$27,000
Average revenue from catering (per booking)*	$90,000	$120,000	$160,000

* This revenue represents the total amount paid by the customer.

Corporate bookings

I have been approached by the Managing Director of ABC, a wind turbine manufacturer with a large research & development facility in a remote part of SK. Although the research positions are highly sought after, the isolated location is a considerable source of frustration to the staff who move there. Retaining the best researchers in this environment is proving challenging, and ABC is looking for ways to incentivise key staff (and their families) to stay.

The proposed arrangement is very simple. V will notify ABC of any package holidays that are undersubscribed. ABC will then advertise these holidays to staff, highlighting the discount available. This is a win-win-win situation: we win because we sell more holidays and have our holidays promoted to more people; ABC wins because they are seen to be a caring employer who is going the extra mile for its staff; ABC's staff win because they think they're getting a unique promotion.

Due to their isolated location, few (if any) of the ABC's research & development staff will be familiar with V's branches and so will be none the wiser that what they are being offered is no different to what any V customer could get. Furthermore, the Managing Director has agreed to let me have the names and addresses of his staff so that we can target them directly with promotional material.

Conclusion

Each of these opportunities above gives us a valuable opportunity to increase both revenue and market share for V. I can see no reason why we should not take full advantage of all three of them.

End of report

Where a cost of capital is required to assess projects, V uses a standard rate of 10%.

Required

(a) With reference to the current product range only, **advise** the board how V might be able to achieve sustainable competitive advantage as defined by Professor Michael Porter. **(12 marks)**

(b) **Calculate** the potential financial benefits of the Care Holiday and Conference proposals and **advise** the board of any issues that need to be considered when using the figures for decision-making purposes.

Note: There are 10 marks available for calculations

(15 marks)

(c) Use Ansoff's product market scope matrix to **evaluate** the three alternative strategies proposed by the IT Director. **(15 marks)**

(d) With reference to the CIMA code of ethics, **discuss** the ethical issues that should be considered when evaluating the new proposals. **(8 marks)**

(Total marks for question = 50 marks)

BPP
LEARNING MEDIA

Question 3

V – Travel Business

Unseen case material

The growth of V's online business in recent years has prompted concern within the company about the long term viability of V's high street branches.

Although V offers a discount to customers who buy holidays through its online bookings (pre-seen page 3), the net operating profit margin (%) from the high street branches is still lower than that for online bookings, due to the operating costs associated with the high street branches. A number of branches have also reported a decline in the overall number of customer bookings in recent years, although the number of prestige holidays booked through the branches has remained largely constant.

V's revenues for its different products are split between high street branches and online bookings as follows (based on the actual results to 30 June 2012):

	Package	Adventure	Prestige	Support
	%	%	%	%
High street	20	21	70	60
Online	80	79	30	40

The gross margins V earns on the different products sold in its branches and online are:

	Package	Adventure	Prestige	Support
	%	%	%	%
High street	30	25	45	30
Online	25	20	35	25

V's operating costs for the year ended 30 June 2012 can be summarised as:

Staff costs: SK $ 16.5 million – of which 75% relate directly to the high street branches

Marketing costs: SK $11 million – of which 80% relate directly to the cost of printing and distributing promotional literature for the high street branches

Other operating and administration costs (eg rates, utilities etc.) SK $14.5 million – of which 70% relate directly to the high street branches.

Rationalisation of branch network

The performance of the high street stores compared to V's online business was discussed at the length at the last Board meeting, where the IT Director suggested he thought V would be better to sell all of its high street stores and focus on online trading instead. For example, he suggested that if V sold the freeholds for some of the shops it currently owns, this money could be used to fund the purchase a new search and reservation system, which is faster and has significantly greater capacity than V's current system. According to the IT Director, this new system would allow V to expand its online business.

Product types and strategy

However, the Operations Director warned against making what he called 'any over-hasty strategic decisions' based on these overall figures.

He suggested that V needs to look in more detail at the types of customers who buy the different types of holiday product, to ensure that any strategy it devises will fit with their needs and requirements such that they continue to use V to book their holidays.

The Operations Director reminded the other Directors that the key characteristics of the three product markets are as follows:

Package – Although there is a wide variety of destinations, the basic package product itself is fairly standardised. There is intensive competition in this market, and it is fairly price sensitive.

Adventure travel – This market caters primarily for young adults who are highly price sensitive, and who are also active users of social media.

Prestige – customers tend to be older, and are looking for higher value holidays. These customers tend to be relatively insensitive to price, but they often want holidays in more exotic locations, or holidays which are linked to special events or interests. Many of these customers still prefer to buy holidays face-to-face rather than online.

In relation to this, the Finance Director reiterated the point that she felt some products may be more profitable than others. Therefore, she argued that V should be looking to focus on the most profitable products, and she asked the other directors to consider what impact closing all of V's high stores would be likely to have on its product mix and profitability overall. The Finance Director said she accepted that it may be necessary to close some of V's high street branches, but any such decisions should be taken after looking at the mix of products sold and the profitability of the individual stores in question.

The Executive Chairman also said he would be very reluctant to close all of V's shops because the 'personal touch' which the shop staff could give was an important part of the customer service which V offered its customers. This, he said, played an important part in V's high customer satisfaction rating (pre-seen page 4), and it was particularly valued by customers booking 'Prestige' travel holidays.

Moreover, the Executive Chairman questioned whether closing the shops would really allow V to expand and diversify its holiday product range and provide more choice to customers, which he felt was what V should be trying to achieve.

Following these discussions in the board meeting, the Human Resources Director also pointed out: 'Whatever we decide, we need to ensure that any changes are handled carefully, and communicated effectively to our staff and customers. I am concerned that any negative publicity surrounding job losses will get in the way of our expansion plans.'

Industry coverage in the press

Shortly after the Executive Chairman's statement about the importance of customer service – quoted in the national press in January 2012 (pre-seen page 4) – one of the national newspapers in SK published an article which suggested that only 10% of people booking their annual holiday now use a high street travel shop, as most opt to organise their trip online. The article argued that people are increasingly using internet search engines and review websites (like TripAdvisor) to research and book their own holidays. A significant number of consumers enjoy being able to put together their own holiday on the internet.

The newspaper article highlighted that the internet has made researching a holiday much easier than it used to be, and the growth of review sites indicates that people are increasingly trusting the opinion of their peers when selecting their holiday destination. The article quoted findings from a recent nationwide survey in SK which found that only about 15% of customers now believe that travel agents are better informed about holiday destinations than blogs or review websites they could refer to themselves. As a result, travel agent 'brands' – either on the high street or on their own websites – are becoming less important for customers than they used to be.

The article also noted that a key factor in the shift in consumer attitudes was price; with over half of consumers believed that holidays are better value for money when booked online. The growth of price comparison websites has also made price more important; for example, by allowing consumer to compare the cost of all aspects of a trip, from flights, hotel rooms, to travel insurance and foreign currency rates.

However, the article concluded by noting that 'For more complicated itineraries, or for certain bespoke holidays, there is still a benefit in speaking to a specialist agent in person in a store, or on the telephone, due to the value they can add in booking these complicated trips.'

The Directors discussed the implications of this article, and the Finance Director expressed concern about how V would be able to achieve its objective to grow earnings by an average of 5% a year in such difficult conditions. She said the only opportunities for growth she could see lay in specialist, prestige travel.

Required

(a) **Explain** the benefits that V might gain from conducting a value chain analysis and any limitations which V might face in applying the value chain to its business.

Note: You are not required to draw a value chain diagram as part of your answer to this question.

(14 marks)

(b) (i) **Calculate** the impact of the decision to close all of V's high street branches.

Note: All 6 marks are available for calculations. Ignore the cost of any redundancy payments. **(6 marks)**

(ii) **Evaluate** the proposal to close all of V's high street branches, and the alternative proposal to close only a proportion of the high street branches. **(10 marks)**

(c) **Advise** the directors of the benefits of using environmental analysis to help them to make a decision about the possible branch closures.

Note: You are not required to advise the directors what the decision should be. **(8 marks)**

(d) At the next Board meeting, the Directors are going to debate an initial proposal to close five of V's smaller branches, all of which are located relatively close to a larger branch. Assuming the Directors accept the proposal to close the five branches, **advise** them about:

(i) The issues they should consider when implementing the closures

(ii) How resistance to the closures may be reduced.

(12 marks)

(Total marks for question = 50 marks)

BPP
LEARNING MEDIA

Question 4

V – Travel Business

Unseen case material

Forecast performance

At the last Board meeting, the Finance Director presented an updated forecast for the business, showing that the net operating profit for the year end 30 June 2013 was expected to be SK $35.5 million.

The Finance Director said that, although this figure was below the original budget for the year (of SK $ 37m), she felt V could be satisfied with any growth in profits compared to 2012, given the tough trading conditions. She commented that many of V's competitors were forecasting significant reductions in profits for 2013, and so V is continuing to out-perform them.

However, in the light of these figures, the Operations Director questioned whether V's financial objective to grow earnings by 5% per year on average (pre-seen page 3) was still realistic.

Customer service

The Executive Chairman acknowledged that trading conditions were indeed very tough, but he maintained that he still felt V should be able to grow in the future, by expanding and diversifying its product range in order to provide more variety and choice to customers.

However, the Chairman also reiterated his belief that the cornerstone of V's success, and what makes it unique, is the level of service it offers its customers, based on the knowledge and dedication of its experienced staff.

According to the Chairman: 'V's business strategy will revolve around providing high quality service to our various target customers, thereby fully satisfying all of their needs all of the time. We must offer completely enjoyable holidays which will ensure that travellers are thoroughly satisfied and appreciative at the end of their trips.'

Performance measurement

By the end of the last Board meeting, there was a consensus among the Directors that customer service was crucial to V's future success.

However, the Human Resources director expressed concern that the focus of the Board meetings has increasingly been on financial performance, rather than looking either at any strategic issues or at the operational performance of the business.

He argued that, given the importance of providing high quality service to its customers, V should be measuring how well it is actually providing that service.

The Operations director pointed out that more detailed performance information is available to each of the branch managers, although it is not included in the summary performance reports produced for the Board.

The detailed performance information provided to the branch managers includes:

- Sales revenue by product type and by staff member (which is used when calculating staff bonuses)

- Number of customer enquiries, and the ratio of enquiries to booking

- Number of bookings (analysed into first-time bookings and repeat bookings)

- Churn rate (the % of customers who had previously booked with V(*) but who have not made a booking in the last two years)

- Number of customer complaints

- Customer satisfaction rating(**)

(*): When customers made a booking with V, their details are entered on V's database and remain stored for three years.

(**): V sends out a customer satisfaction questionnaire to all customers after they have been on their holiday, asking them for their feedback on the holiday itself and the selection and booking process.

Staff training

On several occasions, recently, the Operations Director has suggested that if V is going to expand its holiday product range successfully then all the staff who deal with customers will need more product-related training; in particular, training about new products or packages which have become available. He pointed out that if V's staff do not understand the full product portfolio, they will not be able to give customers the level of advice they have come to expect from V.

The Director's concern in this area has come from a drop in the customer satisfaction scores, in particular those relating to 'How knowledgeable were the staff' and 'How well did your holiday meet your requirements.'

The Human Resources Director agreed that V needs to offer its staff more product training. He pointed out if V cannot offer its customers information or advice which they could not otherwise find themselves (for example through an internet search) then V's business model will not be sustainable. In this respect, he said that complex itineraries and/or unusual destinations could actually present opportunities for V to expand, but only if V's staff have the knowledge to be able to advise customers about them.

The IT Director suggested that rather than sending large numbers of staff on a product training course, it may be more efficient to develop an a 'product updates page' on V's intranet system (which is maintained by head office). In this way, branch managers can find out about any new products and then inform their staff of them.

New commission deal

V currently sells very few holidays to country C. Historically, C has not been a popular destination for European holiday-makers but the government and national tourist board of C are keen to promote international tourism in the country.

HN Group

HN Group owns a number of luxury hotels in C, and has recently approached V to help it sell holidays in SK through V's Prestige Travel service. HN has proposed the following deal:

- If V acts exclusively for HN in C, then HN will give V a commission of 4% of the total price of all HN hotel accommodation it sells in C. This commission rate will increase to 5% (of the total annual sales) if V sells more than 22,500 packages per year.

- This exclusive deal will last for five years.

HN pays a commission of 2% to any agents which sell accommodation for other hotel chains in C. If V rejects the exclusive deal, it could still book accommodation packages in HN's hotels, and earn this lower commission rate on these bookings.

The average price of an accommodation package booked at HN hotels in 2011 was SK $ 800.

V's initial market research suggests that it could sell 20,000 packages to HN in the first year, and this figure will rise at 5% per year thereafter.

TL Group

A second hotel chain in country C has also approached V to help sell holidays for it in SK. TL Group has offered V a flat rate commission of 3% on the value of all packages sold in TL hotels in C.

TL Group's hotels are lower quality, and significantly cheaper, than HN's, but V believes they could appeal to younger holiday makers (for example, those who might currently buy an Adventure package.) The average price of an accommodation package at TL hotels in 2011 was SK $450.

V has estimated that it could sell 25,000 packages for TL hotels in the first year, with this figure rising at 3% per year. The difference in market positioning means that any sales V makes to TL will not reduce the amount of sales it could also make to HN.

Neither the TL or HN deal offers V any commission on the flight element of any packages sold.

Sustainable tourism

In recent months, V has noticed an increase in customers wanting to visit Paragonia, a remote destination in a rainforest location.

This increased demand has coincided with increased press coverage about Paragonia. However, the majority of the press coverage has been about deforestation and the environmental damage being caused by tourism in Patagonia. One press article even concluded that 'Tourism destroys the very places it seeks to promote.'

Nonetheless, all the press articles have conceded that the local residents in Paragonia have embraced tourism because it provides them with a valuable source of income.

The Finance Director has expressed some concern about V taking bookings for holidays in Paragonia. She has noted that on V's website the company says: it takes its social responsibility very seriously; strives to ensure that its trips are sustainable as well as authentic; and endeavours only to deal with resorts and hotels which contribute positively to their environments and communities.

Required

(a) **Evaluate** the benefits of V's Board monitoring non-financial aspects of performance as well as financial ones.

Note: You should **not** refer to any specific frameworks of performance measurement (for example, the Balanced Scorecard) in your answer to this part of the question.

(8 marks)

(b) Briefly **explain** the components of the Balanced Scorecard model. **(4 marks)**

(c) **Advise** the Directors:

(i) Of the advantages of introducing the Balanced Scorecard at V **(6 marks)**

(ii) Of THREE potential problems they might encounter if they introduce the Balanced Scorecard. **(6 marks)**

(d) **Recommend**, with reasons, whether or not V should accept the *exclusive deal* being offered by HN.

Ignore the time value of money in any calculations, and assume that the average price of accommodation remains at 2011 levels.

Note: There are 9 marks available for calculations in requirement (d).

(18 marks)

(e) **Discuss** the corporate social responsibility issues relating to the rainforest holidays. **(8 marks)**

(Total marks for question = 50 marks)

Question 5

V – Travel Business

Unseen case material

The directors of V are concerned that V's results have been slow to improve, despite the heavy investment in its online operations five years ago, in Sept 2007 (ie impacting earnings in year ending 30 June 2008).

In an attempt to improve V's medium term prospects, the directors are looking for attractive investment opportunities which expand their product portfolio. In particular, they are considering the relative merits of:

- launching luxury cruise holidays, which would be sold as a 'Prestige Travel' product, and
- the acquisition of a small chartered airline.

For operational reasons it will not be possible to invest in both projects at the same time.

Financial data for V

Extracts from the group financial statements for 2012 are provided on page 6 of the Pre-seen. Financial objectives can be found on page 3.

Additional data is provided below:

Year ended 30 June	2007	2008	2009	2010	2011	2012
Number of shares in issue throughout the year (million)	85.0	90.0	90.0	90.0	90.0	90.0
earnings per share (SK cents*)	28.0	23.0	25.0	26.3	27.0	26.7
dividend per share	22.4	4.6	20.0	19.7	19.7	19.7

100 SK cents per SK$

Cruise holidays

V has been approached by Cabaret S.A. (hereafter Cabaret), a large established French cruise operator who is now aiming to grow its cruise business in SK, the country that V is based in. The cruise market is a growing part of the holiday market, but is already highly competitive. Estimates of the outcome of this project vary considerably according to, for example, assumptions made about the state of the economy in SK which might be either successfully emerging from recession (scenario A) or might continue to stagnate (scenario B).

To date SK$ 0.2 million has been spent on initial market research and contract negotiations.

Cabaret have proposed a commercial venture which entitles V to sell cruise holidays on Cabaret's vessels from 1 January 2013 on the following terms:

- V would incur one-off higher levels of advertising expenditure costing SK$ 3 million; this cost is tax-deductible. V would also be required to invest in a new call centre, costing SK$ 6.75m. These costs would be the same under either **scenario A** or **scenario B** and would be paid on 1 January 2013.
- V would be responsible for investing in high levels of customer support including organising chartered trains to transport customers from key cities to the ports from which the cruises will operate. The costs of chartering trains and other operating costs are estimated for 2013 at:
  - SK$ 2 million under **scenario A**
  - SK$ 1.5 million under **scenario B**.

- V would pay to reserve a block of holidays from Cabaret, this amount is not refundable if V does not sell the holidays. The cost in 2013 will be EUR 1 million.

- V estimates the potential revenue in 2013 to be:
  - SK$ 7.35 million under **scenario A**
  - SK$ 3.68 million under **scenario B**.

- All operating costs can be assumed to rise by 5% per year, and revenue by 3 % per year.

It can be assumed that if scenario A occurs in 2013 it will also occur in all subsequent years. The same is true with scenario B. It is estimated that there is a 70% probability of occurrence for scenario A and a 30% probability of scenario B.

Other relevant financial information for the cruise investment:

- V uses a cost of capital of 15% to evaluate investments of this level of risk.

- The proposed new call centre for the cruise proposal is expected to have a residual value of SK$ 4 million after 4 years.

- Corporate income tax is charged at 30% on taxable profits and is paid at the end of the year in which the taxable profit arises. Tax depreciation allowances are available on all capital expenditure associated with the project at a rate of 100%. Balancing charges will arise on any residual value.

- Operating cash flows should be assumed to arise at the end of the year to which they relate unless otherwise stated.

- The exchange rate is expected to be EUR/SK$ 1.2000 (EUR 1 = SK$ 1.2000) on 1 January 2013 and the Euro is expected to strengthen against the SK dollar by 2% a year in each of the next 4 years.

- The project could be abandoned on 1 January 2014 and the call centre sold for an estimated SK$5.7 million. If the project were abandoned on 1 January 2014, no further cash inflows or outflows would arise from then onwards and there would be no penalties for pulling out of the market.

Acquisition of chartered airline

V has been concerned about its exposure to prise rises from third party operators. Recently V has been in discussion with AirPalma, a chartered airline with operations across Europe that is keen to raise money by disposing of peripheral routes and is keen to pull out of SK for this reason. AirPalma have let it be known that a bid of SK$ 15 million would be enough to secure their operations in SK as a going-concern. V has estimated that this will deliver an NPV of SK$ 5 million.

Required

(a) (i) **Calculate**, for each of the years 2007-2012 inclusive, V's dividend payout ratio and total earnings (SK$m)   **(5 marks)**

(ii) **Evaluate** V's financial performance over this period. Include reference to V's earnings objective.

Up to 3 marks are available for additional calculations   **(7 marks)**

(iii) **Discuss** the possible rationale behind V's dividend pay-out history.   **(6 marks)**

(b) Assume that you are the Management Accountant of V and have been asked to write a *Report* addressed to Board that will assist it in deciding whether or not to proceed with either of the proposed investments. In your report you are required to:

(i) **Calculate** the NPV of the cruise investment; ignoring the option to abandon the project on 1 January 2014   **(13 marks)**

(ii) **Evaluate** whether or not the cruise investment should be abandoned on 1 January 2014 if Scenario B occurs.   **(6 marks)**

(iii) **Advise** whether to proceed with either the cruise project or the acquisition of the chartered airline.   **(10 marks)**

Additional marks are available for structure and presentation.   **(3 marks)**
(Total = 50 marks)

Question 6

V – Travel Business

Unseen case material

Background

Following the expansion plans announced in the Executive Chairman's statement to the press in January 2012, V has been informally approached by some of its competitors and also major tour operators to discuss the sale of V. The directors have so far rejected these approaches but are now re-considering the possibilities.

Sell-off to A plc

The Operations Director has been doing some research into the travel industry in SK. He has found that over the last 10 year, most of the revenue from 'independent travel' sales has moved away from high street travel businesses to vertically integrated tour operators. These large companies have increasingly taken control over supply and distribution of package and adventure holidays. The major tour operators can now sell their products more quickly and cheaply by going direct to the consumer electronically. At the same time they can develop deeper and lasting customer relationships.

One of the most successful of these vertically integrated operators in terms of profit is A plc, which has differentiated through market segmentation away from the mainstream short-haul market to focus on long-haul and specialist markets, especially in the growing independent sector.

A plc has recently approached V to offer SK\$4.50 per share, on a share for share exchange, for a private trade sale. A plc plans to integrate V into the existing A plc business as a separate trade channel, retaining the existing management.

The Operations Director believes that a trade sale to A plc would allow V to expand its current core offering of Adventure and Prestige Travel products whilst gaining operational savings from the established supply chain offered by A plc.

Initial Public Offering

The Executive Chairman countered this by stating that considerable evidence exists to suggest that the high street has a future, highlighting two major players who have shown an aggressive retailing strategy in SK, each with plans to expand their high street presence significantly over the next 2 years.

V is intending to develop sophisticated software allowing its branches to dynamically package products for customers. Dynamic packaging is a method used in package holiday bookings that allows the travel agent to build a tailored package of flights, accommodation, and car rental instead of offering a pre-defined package. V believes this can enable it to maintain a key competitive advantage over its rivals. The Executive Chairman believes the future of V lies in further appropriate investment in new technology, working closely with niche tour operators and continuing to build on V's competitive differentiation by focusing on specialist markets where core assets such as staff expertise can add value to the customer buying process.

This would require a substantial future investment in marketing and IT/IS resources and to expand its branch network. The Executive Chairman wants the Board to consider an Initial Public Offering (IPO), that is, a stock market flotation.

Financial data for the proposal

Financial information for A plc, ignoring potential synergistic benefits arising from the possible acquisition of V by A plc:

- There are 100 million SK\$1 shares currently in issue
- Current share price is SK\$43.50 ex div
- Dividend payout is 70% and the latest dividend is expected to be in line with this
- P/E Ratio today is 37
- Latest earnings were SK\$ 119 million

- The gearing level of A plc is approximately the industry average at 10%
- Growth in earnings and dividends is estimated to continue at its historic rate of 7% for the foreseeable future.

Other relevant financial information

A plc expects to be able to use its good reputation and strong market presence to enhance the prospects of V by improving V's annual earnings by 10% from the date of acquisition onwards. This assumes that no new long term capital is raised.

From their experience of previous acquisitions, A plc estimates that integration costs will be SK$10m (pre-tax) in the first year of acquisition, SK$7m (pre-tax) in the second year and a further SK$1m (pre-tax) from the third year onwards to bring the systems and processes in line with general operations of A plc.

The estimated post-tax return on the market is 8% and the risk free rate is 3% and these rates are not expected to change in the foreseeable future. Assume a debt beta of zero.

Proxy plc also operates in the travel industry and has 70 retail outlets throughout SK. Proxy plc maintains a dividend payout ratio of 60%, and has a P/E ratio today of 13 and an equity beta of 1.4. Gearing is stable at 15% (measured by long term debt divided by long term debt plus equity).

The net book value of buildings, equipment and vehicles of V are considered to reflect their current realisable value.

Required

Assume that you are an external consultant and have been asked to write a report addressed to the Board of V that will assist it in deciding which of the two options should be pursued. In your report you are required to:

(a)   Calculate, stating your assumptions, a range of values for V in total and per share using:

(i) the dividend valuation model, using an appropriate cost of equity based on the data provided for Proxy plc   **(8 marks)**

(ii) the P/E basis   **(3 marks)**

(iii) advise on the relevance and limitations of each method   **(7 marks)**

(b)   Calculate the expected post-merger value and share price of A plc, including the impact of the integration costs (discounted at A plc's estimated cost of equity).   **(12 marks)**

(c)   Discuss your results in part (a) and (b) and advise on an appropriate valuation to use in negotiations with A plc. Consideration should be made of the valuation involving a share exchange compared with a proposed share value for an IPO.   **(7 marks)**

(d)   Advise the Directors of V on the advantages and disadvantages of a stock market listing versus a trade sale. Recommend, with reasons, which option to pursue   **(10 marks)**

In addition up to 3 marks are available for structure and presentation.   **(3 marks)**
(Total = 50 marks)

Question 7

V – Travel Business

Unseen case material

It is now 1 December 2012.

The director's of the company have recently held a meeting, where they discussed two issues. The first issue concerned the current incentive scheme for managers, in which bonuses are paid each year if V achieves its financial objective of 5% growth in earnings in that financial year. The directors discussed alternative financial measures that could be used to gauge performance and came up with two proposals

(i)   set a target for asset turnover

(ii)   use a range of financial performance measures which could be compared to an industry benchmark or a competitor

The other issue discussed was the proposed expansion plan. This would involve expanding the range of holidays offered and a greater focus on trading via the Internet. V will offer a new range of last minute deals which are expected to be very popular. To fund the expansion, which will cost SK$15 million to purchase new non-current assets, the directors are proposing to sell six branches which are not profitable and have relatively few bookings taken.

The non-current assets in the branches to be sold off have a net book value of SK$6 million, but it is thought that they can be sold for the amount needed to fund the expansion as negotiations with buyers are already at an advanced stage. The expansion plan would commence on 1 January 2013.

Assume you are assistant to the finance director. You have been asked to provide some key financial data and supporting evidence for discussion by the board. You have so far obtained the following information based on the assumption that the expansion will go ahead.

- Revenue, which is not expected to grow until the commencement of the expansion plan,is expected to grow by 3 per cent per year for the first three years of the expansion. This increased level of sales is then expected to be at least maintained in the following years.

- The ratio of operating costs to revenues will increase by 1 percentage point (from the current percentage) in the year ended 30 June 2013 and by a further 1% in the year ended 30 June 2014 as a increased costs, which V does not feel able to fully pass on to the consumer due to the economic situation. These increased costs outweigh the benefits of lower overheads for V through online sales.

- Redundancy payments resulting from the sale of branches are expected to be SK$2 million which would all be paid during January 2013.

Other relevant information is as follows.

There are no plans to issue additional equity or increase long-term borrowings to fund the expansion plan.

No other sales of non-current assets are planned for the next two years. Total depreciation charged for the year ended 30 June 2012 was SK$8 million. The changes to non-current assets will means that the charge for the year ended 30 June 2013 is SK$4.5 million and for the year ended 30 June 2014 is $5.5million.

Note: this is already included in the change in operating costs above.

Dividends are payable in the year after they are declared. The dividend paid for the year ended 30 June 2012 was SK$19.5 million and was paid in August 2012. It is believed that this total amount will be increased by SK$1 million in each of the next three financial years, as directors are looking to be compensated for lower dividends received in previous years.

Assume dividend are declared and paid on the final day of each year.

After the 2012 accounts were finalised, a legal case was settled in which V was ordered to pay further compensation of SK$5 million to travellers affected by travel disruption in 2010 caused by volcanic ash covering large portions of Europe. This was paid in October 2012. No provision had been made for this in the 2011 accounts.

Interest income arise from short-term cash deposits as this amount is not expected to vary significantly for the foreseeable future.

Finance costs are mostly related to the interest payments on the long-term borrowings (SK$3.9 million). The remainder of the balance is due to overdraft charges caused by the volatility of V's cash flows. These overdraft charges are expected to remain relatively unchanged for the foreseeable future.

Inventories relate to holiday brochures, although the reduction in branches will mean that less brochures are required for existing holidays, there will be further brochures required for the expanded range of holidays meaning that inventories are expected to increase by SK$0.7 million as a result of the expansion.

Suppliers are all suffering trading difficulties due to the economic situation. It is thought that many of them will reduce credit terms significantly which will mean trade and other payables is expected to decrease by 20% in the year ended 30 June 2013 and 10% from 2013 levels in the year ended 30 June 2014.

Trade receivables will increase by 6% in the year ended 30 June 2013 and 4% in the year ended 30 June 2014.

Due to the increased popularity of last minute deals, revenue received in advance (current liabilities) is expected to fall by 7.5% in the year ended 30 June 2013 and by a further 1% in the following year.

Non-current revenue received in advance was exceptionally high in the year ended 30 June 2012 and this is expected to fall by SK$0.8 million at 30 June 2013 and remain at this level for the foreseeable future.

Required

(a)   Prepare a report on the impact of the proposed expansion for the board of directors which:

    (i)   **Calculates** a forecast income statement and statement of financial position for the years to 30 June 2013 and 2014 and **comments briefly on** the limitations of the forecast. **(18 marks)**

    (ii)   **Evaluates** the forecast performance at 30 June 2014 in general and specifically against V's financial objectives **(10 marks)**

    (iii)   **Discusses** the capital structure position of V at 30 June 2014 and any need for financing at this date. **(4 marks)**

    (iv)   **Evaluates** potential alternative sources of finance for financing the expansion starting in 2013. **(7 marks)**

(b)   **Discuss** whether the current financial objectives are appropriate for V and whether the proposed alternative financial performance measures to be used by the company for its incentive scheme would be an improvement.

    Note that part b is not part of the report **(8 marks)**

In addition up to 3 marks are available for structure and presentation. **(3 marks)**

(Total = 50 marks)

Question 8

V – Travel Business

Unseen case material

Assume today is 1 December 2012.

Aircraft acquisition

The directors of V have been evaluating a cost saving project. This will involve the acquisition of two twenty-year old second-hand aircraft at a capital cost of SK$3.5 million each. The acquisition of these aircraft will mean that V will be able to save on the cost of using charter airlines on some of its holiday routes.

The aircraft are expected to be in service for five years. The aircraft have a good safety record, but due to their age they are not expected to last longer than five years. The executive chairman is a strong supporter of this idea saying that it will allow V to offer a better service and more choice to its customers, although he acknowledges that V has no experience in the aviation business, and V has decided to proceed with this initiative. The directors are unsure of the most appropriate method of financing this strategic move.

Leasing

The company has been offered a lease contract with total lease payments of SK$1.05 million per annum for five years, payable in advance, with all maintenance, insurance and general running costs of the aircraft being borne by the lessee.

Alternative sources of finance

Alternatively, the aeroplanes could be purchased outright through either existing funds or from an additional bank loan. The bank has offered V a five-year loan denominated in euros, to match the purchase currency, with variable interest payments payable semi-annually six months in arrears at a margin of 1% per annum above a reference six-month SK$ inter-bank rate. The reference six-month SK$ inter-bank rate is forecast to be at a flat rate of 4.2% for each six-month period, for the duration of the loan.

Other details relating to the aircraft acquisition

V pays tax at 30% and expects to make taxable profits in excess of the lease payments, interest charges and tax depreciation allowances arising over the next five years. Tax depreciation on the purchase of the aircraft can be claimed at a rate of 20% at the end of each financial year on a written-down value basis, with a delay of one year between the tax depreciation allowance arising and the deduction from tax paid.

If bought outright, the aircraft are estimated to have a residual value in real cash flow terms, at the end of five years, of 50% of the original purchase price. However the residual value is highly dependent on the state of the airline industry in five years and there is a risk that the residual value could be much lower because if demand for air travel has declined in this period this will mean that there is very little demand in the secondhand market for aircraft of this age.

Wet lease

There is a second leasing option available to V. V could lease the aircraft under what is known as a 'wet lease.' This would mean that the lessor also provides the crew, fuel, insurance and maintenance for the aircraft throughout the length of the lease. This lease also contains a break clause for V after 3 years.

Post completion audit

The finance director believes that a significant project of this size will require a post-completion audit to be carried out. The executive chairman is not aware of what is involved in a post-completion audit or why it would be necessary to have one. He has requested an explanation of the benefits and drawbacks of a post-completion audit and wants to know whether it would be beneficial for V to make use of them in general.

Financing in euros

Following the consideration of this offer by the directors, it has been discovered that V has another option where it could instead buy similar secondhand aircraft of roughly the same age and quality from a nearby European country

which does use the euro as its currency. These aircraft would be only slightly more expensive than the proposed SK purchase, but the transaction would be denominated in euros.

The operations director has stated if this purchase was to go ahead, the finance for the purchase should also be denominated in euros under the matching concept of matching purchases denominated in one currency with finance denominated in the same currency. The operations director noted that the interest rate in the Euro Zone was 2% per annum lower than in SK.

Required

Assume you are a financial adviser to V. Write a report to the Board about the financing of the aircraft acquisition which:

(a) **Calculates**:

    (i)   The compound annualised post-tax cost of debt

    (ii)   The NPV of the lease versus purchase decision at discount rates of both 6% and 7%

    (iii) The breakeven post-tax cost of debt at which V is indifferent between leasing and purchasing the aeroplanes.   **(11 marks)**

    Note: Ignore the wet lease option and the financing in euros option for this part of the question.

(b) (i)   **Recommends**, with reasons, whether V should purchase with a loan or lease the aircraft.

        Your answer should include appropriate calculations of the sensitivity of the lease versus purchase decision to changes in EACH of the following:

    (1)   The reference SK$ inter-bank rate for the duration of the loan

    (2)   The residual value of the aeroplanes   **(15 marks)**

    Note: Ignore the wet lease and the financing in euros option for this part of the question.

  (ii) **Advise** on the suitability of the wet lease option for V   **(6 marks)**

(c) **Discusses** the usefulness of a post-completion audit in general and **recommend** whether it is necessary for V to carry out a post completion audit for the aircraft acquisition and also in general for large projects.   **(8 marks)**

Additional marks available for structure and presentation in parts (a) and (b):   **(3 marks)**

(d) **Discuss** the potential benefits and problems for V of financing an asset in the same currency as the purchase. Refer to the operations director's comments in your answer.   **(7 marks)**

(Total marks for question = 50 marks)

Question 9

V – Travel Business

Unseen case material

New product range

Following the Executive Chairman's intention to provide more choice to customers by expanding and diversifying V's current holiday product range, the company has decided to launch a new product range called "Events". Excited by the tourism generated at the recent London 2012 Olympic and Paralympic Games, the Executive Chairman has devised this range specifically to attract people who wish to attend major sporting, cultural and other events across the world, such as football tournaments, cricket and cycling tours, athletics meetings, religious gatherings, music and film festivals and even viewing meteorological phenomena such as the Aurora Borealis.

The "Events" range will offer all-inclusive products that cover travel, accommodation, catering, tickets to individual events, associated activities (such as attending practice sessions for sports events, attending social gatherings and visiting local attractions) plus a guide to accompany customers at their events. The Executive Chairman is especially excited about the employment of event guides as he believes that, to turn these into premium products, each event should offer a famous guide – ex-sportsmen and women, film-critics, musicians and other celebrities. He sees the introduction of the "Events" range as his legacy to V, so he is very keen to get the new range launched before he departs in June 2013. Staff will be briefed on this new range by means of the existing Update newsletters that V issues to staff on new products or changes in existing products.

New Information strategy

The planned expansion of V's product range has led the Board to consider whether its existing IT and IS functions are still able to support the company, both now and in the future. Although it made substantial investment in information technology five years ago, this was mostly just to provide an online presence, which allows web users to access details of a V holiday without the need to visit one of V's branches. Holidays can be booked online but because they still require manual processing at V's head office, they are always subject to confirmation within 48 hours of the booking before it can be considered final. Processing includes direct confirmation with the hotel that capacity still exists and with the airline that seats are still available. Head office staff also make sure that no travel warnings are in place for any of the more exotic locations booked.

Branch bookings are taken by sales staff who complete an order form in triplicate. The top copy is given to the customer, the second stays at the branch and the third is scanned and emailed to head office where the same 48 hour processing occurs as with online orders.

Deposits are taken when the booking is first made (both online and in branch) and can be paid for either by debit or credit card. Some branches still accept cash although this is becoming less popular with customers. In most cases, holiday bookings are processed satisfactorily and deposits get allocated to the customer's account. This is done by completing a deposit receipt form which is used to update the head office sales system and then sent to the accountancy team who use it to reconcile the company's bank account and maintain the company's sales ledger.

Once bookings have been successfully processed, head office sales staff inform customers by telephone or email and then match bookings with the head office sales system's record of deposits received. This system produces sales activity reports for the Operations Director and sales reports which are then emailed to the accountancy team for reconciliation with the sales ledger.

Head office sales staff then record the date that customers are due to pay the balance of their holiday on a diary. Each week, a summary of all balances due is emailed out to branches for customers who booked in person. Online customers are emailed with a similar request for payment. All sums due are collected and processed in the same way as deposits.

The management accountant uses the sales ledger information supplied by head office to produce a board report for the Finance Director which analyses sales by product type, location and value.

BPP
LEARNING MEDIA

Product profitability issues

The Finance Director has raised concerns over the profitability of certain products, as the current management information available only records average revenue per booking for each product range. Although the "Package" range of holiday products tends to deliver the most revenue, he is sure that certain products are subsidising others but does not have the data to confirm this. "Adventure" holidays have seen a recent decline in overall bookings but revenue has remained stable, while "Prestige Travel" holidays have remained steady in terms of revenue and bookings.

He is frustrated by the lack of data and has decided to deliver a report to the board that will explain how information on profitability could be captured and reported in order to aid decision-making and increase the company's profits. He has asked you as the company's part-qualified management accountant to draft some ideas for him.

Required

(a)   Considering the Executive Chairman's plan to introduce the "Events" product range:

   (i) **Evaluate** the risks that V faces by introducing the "Events" range by June 2013; *and*   **(12 marks)**

   (ii) **Recommend** controls that V should use to mitigate such risks.   **(8 marks)**

(b)   **Advise** the board on the likely contents of V's new Information Strategy, based on your understanding of how it should be improved. Your answer should use the following three elements (*marks are awarded equally across these elements*):

   (i) Information Systems;

   (ii) Information Technology; *and*

   (iii) Information Management.

   Note: you should assume that V's product range will expand but you do not need to give specific details of how the new system would process sales and bookings.   **(15 marks)**

(c)   **Draft** extracts for the Finance Director's board report that do the following:

   (i) **Recommend** quantitative methods that might be useful in analysing the profitability of V's products.   **(8 marks)**

   (ii) **Discuss** qualitative factors that could support a quantitative analysis of V's products' profitability.   **(7 marks)**

   (Total marks for question = 50 marks)

Question 10

V – Travel Business

Unseen case material

Blues Cruise

The Executive Chairman of V has recently been approached by the CEO of Blues Cruise, a Norwegian company that specialises in providing cruises around Scandinavia and Iceland. Blues Cruise is seeking to expand operations to Africa and the Indian Ocean, where it is warmer, and is interested in a joint venture with V, to be called VB Cruises. Blues Cruise is keen to explore synergies with V, such as the use of combined purchasing power for arranging the flights and hotels that would be required for passenger transfers. The CEO is also impressed by V's website and 99% customer rating. Blues Cruise's customer satisfaction rating varies between 75-85% and levels of repeat business are low. The Executive Chairman is keen to accept this offer, feeling that the joint venture will boost revenues, produce savings and diversify risk. The Finance Director is more cautious as he feels the joint venture would mean exposure to additional risks with which V is unfamiliar and would therefore struggle to manage. (Assume V is not based in a Scandinavian country.)

Hotel Barbados

Hotel Barbados is one of a small chain of Caribbean hotels owned by Val-u, which specialises in affordable family package holidays. The Operations Director has been passed several angry letters of complaint from V customers who experienced severe stomach upsets during their stay at Hotel Barbados. Of greater concern however is news of two fatalities during the summer season. In one of these, a man drowned after suffering a heart attack during a late night swim in one of the many outdoor pools at the hotel. The other fatality happened at the end of the season when a small fire broke out in the hotel nightclub and a guest was crushed in the general confusion.

The Operations Director has now received a letter stating that several of the customers affected by what they claim is food poisoning have now formed an action group, aided by a well known consumer organisation based in SK. The Operations Director is worried about the consequences but at the same time feels that V is not responsible for how hotels operate. 'We can't run the hotels for them,' he commented at the following board meeting. 'If hotels are unable to provide a decent service they should face the consequences, not us.' He added that there had not been problems with Val-u until recently, when it had been bought by a hedge fund.

Travel Agency

In view of his impending share sale, the Executive Chairman is keen to expand revenue as much as possible and has proposed the idea of selling holidays on behalf of other companies. This would involve having hard copy brochures for other companies in V branches and access to other companies' systems for details of availability and to reserve places. Once the booking is placed on behalf of the customer, a deposit would be taken and passed to the relevant holiday company. All further responsibility for the holiday would then lie with that holiday company. The Executive Chairman sees this idea as a way of maintaining utilisation of the branch network by selling other products as V's own sales gradually migrate to the internet. Since the holidays would not be provided by V it would not require any increase in capacity, so the Executive Chairman considers that the commission earned would be relatively risk free.

HIPS

To protect consumers in SK, the holiday industry formed a body called the Holiday Industry Protection Scheme (HIPS). Members of this body are entitled to use the HIPS logo on their marketing material and website. However, membership requires adherence to certain standards, breach of which could result in fines or expulsion from the body. Membership of HIPS is considered an important factor for many customers when considering from whom to buy a holiday. The HIPS standards cover all stages of the holiday. Adverts must be accurate and up-to-date, as well as honest and decent. Branches should be accessible under equality regulations. The booking process should be fully documented, with customers made aware of key information such as visa or health requirements. Once bookings are made, alterations to the booking are not allowed unless imposed by circumstances beyond the member's control. There are rules over complaint handling too. Compliance with conditions is monitored by way of an audit by HIPS every two years. In view of the problems at the Val-u chain,

BPP
LEARNING MEDIA

the Operations Director has asked the Head of Internal Audit to assess the likelihood of V retaining its membership of HIPS.

Required

(a)   (i) **Explain** the **additional** risks V faces in entering a joint venture with Blues Cruise. **(12 marks)**

        (ii) **Recommend** controls that V should use to mitigate risks identified in (i) **(12 marks)**

(b)   (i) **Discuss** the extent to which the risks associated with the problems at Hotel Barbados lie with V as opposed to the hotel chain. **(6 marks)**

        (ii) **Advise** V on steps that it should have taken to prevent the problems like those at Hotel Barbados occurring. **(8 marks)**

(c)   **Evaluate** the Executive Chairman's proposal to commence acting as an agent for other holiday companies. **(6 marks)**

(d)   **Recommend** the procedures to be performed by Internal Audit to assess the likelihood of retaining membership of HIPS. **(6 marks)**

(Total marks for question = 50 marks)

Question 11

V – Travel Business

Unseen case material

Change of Chief Executive

Recent ill-health has meant that the Executive Chairman announced his immediate retirement at the last board meeting. The directors unanimously appointed the Operations Director as acting Executive Chairman.

In his speech to the board at this meeting, the acting Executive Chairman outlined the challenges that he believed V faced over the next few years. He acknowledged that V could not afford to stand still, and that it was essential for the company to develop new products. It would have to take account of the greater proportion of holidays booked on-line and perhaps reduce its branch network. However V would also have to undertake costly investment in marketing and information systems for these new products to deliver acceptable growth. He felt that it was inevitable that V would have to seek a listing on the country's stock market for smaller listed companies to order to raise the funds required for substantial investment sometime in the next two years or so. He had already had preliminary discussions with V's professional advisers about the requirements that V would need to fulfil to obtain a listing.

Decisions about the future governance structure of V were deferred until a future board meeting. The acting Executive Chairman however expressed his preference for keeping the structure unchanged, with himself as permanent Executive Chairman, to provide a necessary focus for leadership at the head of the company. The Finance Director raised the possibility of the acting Executive Chairman holding the new position of Chief Executive, with a non-executive Chairman being recruited from outside the company.

Consumer survey

The last board meeting also considered at length the results of a major survey of V's activities by a consumer watchdog body within the travel industry. The watchdog's reports are well-respected within the industry and are also viewed on-line by many consumers.

The watchdog's representatives visited a number of V's branches and also made a number of enquiries on-line. Some branches were rated very highly by the watchdog. However staff at two branches attempted to sell holidays that were not suitable or were clearly not what the 'customers' wanted. When the watchdog's representatives returned to the two branches for a second visit, they were given the same 'hard-sell' treatment by different members of staff. The two branches concerned have been amongst the best recent performers within V at exceeding their sales targets.

The survey also found that some staff working at branches and responding to on-line enquiries seemed to lack knowledge of, or be confused about, holiday packages that V had launched over the previous year.

When the survey was posted onto the watchdog's website, the comments posted by readers were mixed. There was some positive feedback about the level of service that customers had received in V's branches. However there were also negative comments, including further complaints about the two branches identified as 'hard-selling' holidays to the watchdog's representatives.

The acting Executive Chairman commented that the results appeared to be at variance with the recent surveys that V had undertaken internally, which had yielded the 99% satisfaction rating. He felt that V needed to take the comments very seriously, as they could damage V's profitability. He said that one of his first tasks would be to re-assess the ways in which branch performance was measured, in order to address the issues that had been raised. V would also need to review the ways in which staff were told about new holidays that V was introducing.

Insurance cover

The watchdog also found that, at one of the branches where staff appeared to lack knowledge of some of the company's holidays, the staff member to whom its representative talked to appeared to be unclear about the policy cover and exclusions of the insurance policy that he was trying to sell. In addition the acting Executive Chairman had received a few complaints about the selling of insurance by V's staff. Two customers had complained that they had been told incorrectly that taking out insurance was compulsory. One of the customers

had booked his holiday through a branch, the other had gone on-line. In addition another on-line customer had complained that he had not been asked about pre-existing medical conditions. Illness had caused him to cut short his holiday, but the insurers refused to pay out for the costs incurred on the grounds that the illness was clearly related to his medical condition.

One of the customers who complained to V had also contacted the country's financial services authority, which is responsible for overseeing the sale of insurance. The authority's rules state that travel firms have to demonstrate that they are fit and proper and appropriately resourced in order to be given authorisation to sell insurance. The rules require staff to be competent and able to provide customers with clear information about products and services, so that customers can make informed choices.

The authority has contacted V, asking for V's comments on the complaint and also the findings of the survey. A competitor had its authorisation to sell insurance revoked by the authority for a period, until it was able to demonstrate substantial improvements in its procedures.

Currency exchange cards

The Finance Director informed the rest of the board that profitability on the new currency cards had been disappointing. The acting Executive Chairman wondered why this was so, what determined the exchange rates V quoted and whether the cards had any other uses, particularly hedging payments made to suppliers abroad. The Finance Director agreed to carry out a wider-ranging review of how the currency cards fitted into V's product portfolio and the risks associated with them. This would include reviewing the current structure of fees on the card. At present V charges a fee for each foreign currency withdrawal, a redemption fee and an inactivity fee if the card is not used for six months. These fees are common in the travel industry. If customers redeem the card, the exchange rate at which they obtain the original currency is based on market rates at the date of redemption, not the date the card was purchased.

Required

(a) **Discuss** whether the existing leadership structure of V's board should be maintained, or whether the Finance Director's suggestion of recruiting a Chairman from outside V should be adopted. **(13 marks)**

(b) **Recommend,** with reasons, TWO measures that can be used under each perspective in the balanced scorecard to assess the performance of branches. The four measures are Financial; Customer; Learning and growth; Internal business processes. **(12 marks)**

(c) (i) **Evaluate** the ethical and commercial implications if the allegations of mis-selling insurance are found to be justified. **(10 marks)**

 (ii) **Recommend**, with reasons, the actions that V's board should take in order to prevent problems with the selling of insurance occurring in the future. **(6 marks)**

(d) **Advise** the Executive Chairman about the issues he has raised about the currency exchange cards and **evaluate** the other risks associated with the operation and commercial development of the cards.

(9 marks)

(Total marks for question = 50 marks)

Question 12

V – Travel Business

Unseen case material

Investment in hotel

Over the summer season, V has faced a number of problems in the resort for which it sells the most package holidays. The number of hotels in this resort has previously been limited by local planning regulations. Not all of the hotels meet the quality standards of V and other tour operators, and as a result there has been a lot of competition amongst travel operators for those that do reach the required standard. On four occasions during the summer season, customers of V arrived at their hotels, only to find that their rooms were occupied by holidaymakers who had booked through a competitor. V's customer representative had great difficulty relocating its customers and most were forced to move to inland hotels because all the other hotels at the resort were fully booked. V was forced to pay compensation and received significant adverse coverage in the media.

The government of the country where the resort is located has announced that it is relaxing planning regulations in the area and will allow more hotels to be built, in order to stimulate the local economy. V's board has therefore decided to invest SK$6m in the construction and development of a new hotel. The board intends that the hotel will supply most of the company's accommodation requirements in future seasons and will also be used to build demand from holidaymakers from the country where it is located. V's board wishes to develop the hotel on its own and does not wish to be involved with a local joint venture partner, although the government has indicated that it would prefer local firms to take advantage of development opportunities at the resort.

Financing of hotel

Although V had a substantial cash surplus at its June 2012 year-end, it has subsequently been used to pay a dividend in line with V's financial objectives. V's board has also decided that when the Executive Chairman retires in June 2013, V should buy back the shares that he is selling so that the current directors can maintain control of the company. The Executive Chairman is drawing up plans for developing other products before he leaves. V's board has also agreed that there should be further investment in V's information systems, in response to increasingly urgent requests from the Operations and IT Directors.

V's Finance Director is therefore investigating financing the cost of constructing the hotel by a loan over 10 years from early in 2013. He is looking into two possibilities:

- Obtaining a loan in the country where the hotel will be situated. Interest rates in the country have recently fallen, as part of its government's drive to stimulate economic activity.

- Undertaking a currency swap. The swap would be arranged through a bank in the country where the hotel would be built. The regit, R, is the local currency in that country. The Finance Director has identified a possible arrangement where V would borrow SK$6 million in its home country at a rate of 8% and its swap partner would borrow R30 million at a rate of 6%. The current spot rate is SK$1 = R5 and the SK$ is expected to weaken by 3% each year against the R for the 10 years that both loans would last. The two companies would swap the principal sums at the start of the loan period and then each pay the interest on each other's borrowing. Both of the proposed loans would be repayable in one lump sum at the end of the borrowing period. The other board members have requested more details about the financial effects of the swap.

Premium package

V's board is also considering the package that the new hotel should offer customers. The all-inclusive packages it has sold in other resorts that include all meals and drinks have been very popular with customers. The Operations Director has proposed that V's new hotel should offer premium, all-inclusive deals that will be more expensive than the deals that it has previously sold at that resort. Such all-inclusive deals are not currently offered by other hotels in that resort or in other resorts nearby.

Problems with travel representatives

The customer representative who had to deal with the accommodation problems over the summer has been commended by V's board for dealing as well as possible with very difficult circumstances. However, over the summer season V has had complaints about five of its other customer representatives. Complaints have alleged that representatives are never available when required and discourteous, and also spend all their time talking to young and good-looking holidaymakers and ignoring other customers. Complaints about four of the representatives have been made to V's head office and one has been passed back by the customer representative's line manager. (Line managers supervise customer representatives in a number of resorts, are organised in regions of varying sizes, and are based in a popular resort within their region.) The Finance Director has also reported that the expenses claimed by some of these representatives, and other representatives as well, have increased significantly compared with previous seasons.

The Executive Chairman has reacted with dismay to these allegations. He has emphasised the importance of customer representatives in giving V's customers the holiday experiences that they desire. He has proposed that internal audit staff be sent out posing as customers to review what representatives are doing. The Head of Internal Audit is sceptical about the usefulness of monitoring representatives on-site compared with its costs and usage of audit staff time, but has agreed to consider how to choose which representatives to investigate.

Required

(a) (i) **Evaluate** the risks to V arising from the construction and operation of the hotel, excluding the risks relating to the premium all-inclusive deals. **(10 marks)**

　　(ii) **Recommend** controls that V should operate over the construction of the hotel. **(8 marks)**

(b) (i) **Discuss** the issues arising from financing the development of the hotel by borrowing in regits. **(7 marks)**

　　(ii) **Calculate** the net present value of V's cash flows associated with financing if it accepts the swap arrangements that have been identified. Assume a required discount rate of 8%. **(9 marks)**

(c) **Evaluate** the risks to V arising from the sale of premium all-inclusive deals at the hotel and **recommend** methods by which the risks can be monitored and controlled. **(10 marks)**

(d) **Discuss** the criteria that internal audit can use to select which customer representatives to investigate.

(6 marks)

(Total marks for question = 50 marks)

ANSWERS

Question 1

Marking scheme

Marks

Requirement (a)

Definition of mission statement	1
Explanation of what constitutes an effective mission statement	
Up to three marks for each point explained and then evaluated in the context of V	
Factors include (but are not limited to):	

- Impacts on individual's behaviour
- Reflect the distinctive advantage of the organisation
- Is realistic and attainable
- Is flexible to the demands of a changing environment — Up to 12

MAXIMUM FOR REQUIREMENT — <u>**12**</u>

Requirement (b)

Up to two marks per well justified objective using Balanced Scorecard headings
[Credit will be given for using other models (eg the Performance Pyramid) as long as a reasonable range of objectives is given]
Financial, internal, customer and learning/growth
Objectives need to be specific, measureable, achievable, relevant and time-bound

MAXIMUM FOR REQUIREMENT — <u>**8**</u>

Requirement (c)(i)

Analysis of concerns of internal stakeholders:
    Finance Director, Operations Director, Marketing Manager, HR Director
1 mark for clarifying source of concern
1 mark for advising on action to manage

MAXIMUM FOR REQUIREMENT — <u>**8**</u>

Requirement (c)(ii)

Analysis of the concerns of two other stakeholders:
    suppliers, customers, Operations department staff, temporary staff
For each stakeholder analysed:
1 mark for clarifying source of concern
1 mark for advising on action to manage — <u>**4**</u>
No extra given for discussing more than two stakeholders

MAXIMUM FOR REQUIREMENT

Requirement (d)

<u>Calculations</u>

Recovery of lost revenue	2
Saving of staff costs	1
Hiring of extra temporary staff	½
Hardware costs	½
Software licences	1
Training costs	1
NPV calculation @ 6%	<u>1</u>
MAXIMUM FOR CALCULATIONS	7

BPP
LEARNING MEDIA

<u>Commentary</u>
Up to 2 marks per well-explained point linked directly to the scenario. Issues include:

- Positive NPV, but only with sales recovery – is this realistic?
- No mention of redundancy costs, which will reduce NPV
- No consultation of colleagues to validate figures (eg operations staff)
- No licences allocated to non-operating staff (what about other users e.g. Finance?)
- Heavy reliance on figures from MNO – need other tenders for comparison

Up to 9

Recommendation
1 mark for making a clear recommendation to adopt project   1
1 mark for relating recommendation to issues discussed below   1
MAXIMUM FOR REQUIREMENT   **Max 18**

TOTAL FOR QUESTION   <u>50</u>

Suggested solution

(a)   A mission statement is a published statement of an organisation's fundamental reason for existing expressed in general terms. It describes the basic purpose of an organisation and what it is trying to accomplish.

Lynch provides four criteria against which the effectiveness of a mission statement can be judged:

<u>Impact on individuals' behaviour</u>
The mission statement needs to be specific enough to impact on individuals' behaviour. It should act as a permanent reminder to each member of staff to help them prioritise everyday decisions. If the mission statement is brief and memorable, staff are more likely to remember and refer to it.

The Executive Chairman's mission statement is brief enough to be memorable. It would be entirely reasonable to expect staff to be able to quote it when making decisions. However, although the statement gives a clear expectation (expand and diversify), it fails to address how this should be achieved. As an extreme example, the mission statement could technically be achieved by launching a wide range of unprofitable, unpopular products.

<u>Reflect the distinct advantage of the organisation</u>
When it comes to competing, an organisation needs to be clear as to why its customers choose it. By incorporating this into the mission statement, the organisation ensures that any source of competitive advantage is retained and exploited wherever possible.

According to the Executive Chairman, V's source of competitive advantage is its "particular attention to customer service" in the form of "friendly, direct, personal service". Although there is recognition in V's mission statement of providing choice to customers, this is not linked directly to the level of service. So, for example, the product range could be expanded dramatically at the cost of personal customer service. This would meet the mission statement but work against a source of V's competitive advantage.

<u>Be realistic and attainable</u>
For staff to buy into the mission statement, they need to believe that it is challenging but achievable. If it is felt to be idealistic, it will be disregarded as impractical when it comes to decision-making.

V's mission statement should be very easy to achieve, in that it demands more choice for its customers. With only three types of product in its current portfolio, V has a vast range of potential new products to choose from. The issue as to whether this will be profitable or increase market share is a serious omission from the mission statement which makes it easy to deliver but unlikely to benefit V as a whole.

<u>Be flexible to the demands of a changing environment</u>
For a mission statement to be effective, it needs to be incorporated into the organisation's culture. This takes time and it is therefore appropriate for a mission statement to be kept for at least a few years. If this is the case, the mission statement needs to be flexible enough to remain relevant as the external environment will inevitably change over that period.

V's mission statement is very broad, in that it does not restrict V to any specific markets, products or distribution channels which may come into or fall out of fashion. As a result, it provides full flexibility to react to whatever may happen in the external environment. However, as discussed above, the mission statement is so flexible that it gives little direction.

(b)   In order to provide an appropriate range of objectives, Balanced Scorecard headings have been used:

Financial
To maintain the overall net margin at its current rate of 14%.
The Executive Chairman describes V as having "a comparatively high level of revenues and operating profit". An objective to maintain the net margin at 14% ensures that any increases in market share (see Customer perspective below) are not offset by excessive cost increases.

Customer
To increase market share by 5% per annum for each of the next five years.
The Executive Chairman has made it clear that he wants V to expand and diversity. This objective will ensure that V offers new products that are attractive to its current and potential customers.

Learning and growth
To provide each member of sales staff with two days training per annum in V's product range.
V does not currently offer product-based training to staff on the basis that they "will become familiar with such product details as they gain experience". This approach could undermine the ability of staff to sell effectively as the range expands.

[Tutorial note: an objective focusing on the learning aspect of the Balanced Scorecard (e.g. to launch at least two new products each year) would be equally appropriate here. However, marks under the "learning & growth" heading are capped at 2.]

Internal business
To reduce the number of holidays cancelled due to lack of availability to no more than 1% of total bookings by December 2013.
This recognises the problem highlighted in the scenario where customers make a booking which then has to be cancelled because V's systems were not efficiently linked to the holiday providers. This will incentivise investment in internal processes to improve the situation.

[Tutorial note: Students will need to include figures and timescales to make the objective SMART. As long as the values are not entirely unrealistic, they will be given credit]

(c) (i) Finance Director
The Finance Director sounds exasperated at the lack of management information currently available. As a result of previous problems, she has set very low expectations of V's processes. She will not be able to do her job properly unless she gets better management information.

The IT Director should clarify to the Finance Director that, given the current state of technology in society if not in V itself, there is no reason why she shouldn't receive the information she needs. He should explain how the new system will enable a higher volume of information to be processed faster and more accurately, and that this information can easily be shared and analysed by the Finance department. Given this prospect, the Finance Director is likely to become a strong advocate of the new system.

Operations Director
The Operations Director appears to be a bit of a technophobe. He has reached the conclusion that IT is unreliable and can only be controlled with external human intervention. This belief may be strengthened by the fact that the new system would result in redundancies within his department which can be difficult and unpleasant to have to manage.

The IT Director needs to demonstrate that a good IT system is more accurate than human processing, and that highly effective controls can be implemented. It may be worth exploring why previous IT projects failed (e.g. lack of training / user involvement etc) and demonstrate how the new system will be different. There may also be an opportunity to involve the HR Director in managing redundancies. Ultimately, however, the Operations Director needs to be made to face up to the inevitable changes that IT is bringing.

Given his resistance to technology, it is questionable whether the Operations Director should be in charge of internet-based orders. In perceiving it as a process like any other, he is failing to take advantage of the unique opportunities that online selling can provide. It may be appropriate for him to focus on branch-based operations and transfer responsibility for internet orders to the IT director.

HR Director

The HR Director is entirely correct that there are costs involved with the new system and that these can be considerable. However, it is entirely reasonable to expect the HR department to advise on these sorts of issues and, if the business need dictates, take the necessary action.

The HR Director has not expressed any direct resistance to the new system, only that the costs need to be understood. In the context of the IT Director's omission of redundancy costs, this is an entirely reasonable concern. The IT Director therefore needs to ask for the HR Director's professional guidance at this point and incorporate it into the overall plan.

Marketing Manager

The Marketing Manager has evidence that the current website is "quite boring". Given this, and the absence of any e-marketing V is clearly behind its competitors. It is entirely understandable, therefore, that the Marketing Manager wants investment in these activities.

The IT Director firstly needs to make the Marketing Manager see that his project does not mean that no investment can be made in marketing. On the contrary, it can be seen as a first step towards improving the overall customer experience. This can be illustrated by considering what would happen if the Marketing Manager undertook a successful campaign with the existing operations systems in place. This would result in an increased level of customer dissatisfaction and poor reputation. Put simply, a customer would be more forgiving of a boring website than an unreliable booking system.

Furthermore, the new system could give the Marketing Manager very valuable information about V's customers. This could be used as a basis for a more focused (and therefore, potentially, more effective) marketing campaign.

(c) (ii) Suppliers

It is clear that suppliers are currently frustrated by V's archaic systems. It is entirely likely, therefore, that V's bookings are given less attention and priority than others who use more modern booking systems. This is likely to damage V's reputation and competitive position (if it hasn't done already).

The IT director should contact key suppliers and explain the plans ahead. Given their exasperation with the current system, it is highly unlikely that the suppliers will resist this. However, it will be important to ensure that V's new system is compatible with the suppliers' systems and discussions in this area should be entered into as part of the planning stage. It would also be worth keeping them informed of progress on the project in the hopes that they will be supportive and understanding if and when there are any teething problems with the new system.

Customers

Customers are not currently aware of the inefficient manual processes that are being adopted by V, and it would be unwise to bring this to their attention. It would also be unwise to communicate the fact that some customers don't have their bookings honoured.

However, there is potential to highlight that new booking processes are in being implemented that will "make the booking process even faster and more efficient". It could be presented "as part of V's ongoing drive towards providing the best possible customer service". If resources and agreement could be obtained to upgrade the website, it would be good to communicate this to customers as part of the overall message.

There will, inevitably, be teething problems with the new system but, for the same reasons described above, this should not be communicated to customers in advance in the way it would be to suppliers. However, it would be appropriate to have a contingency plan in place (e.g. resorting to the manual process) so that the disruption to the customer is kept to an absolute minimum.

[Tutorial note: Other stakeholders such as Operations department employees and temporary staff could be discussed for equal credit.]

(d)

	T0	T1	T2	T3	
Number of users at start of year T0 = 13 permanent staff + 3 temps T1 - 2 = 8 permanent staff	16	8	8		1 mark
	SK$000	SK$000	SK$000	SK$000	
Recover margin on lost revenue $250M x 60% / 0.003 x 14% margin		63.0	63.0	63.0	2 marks
Save staff costs T0 = 5 staff x $20k x 9 / 12 months T1 - 3 = 5 staff x $20k		75.0	100.0	100.0	1 mark
Extra temporary staff T0 = 3 staff x $20k x 3 / 12 months	(15.0)				½ mark
Hardware	(250.0)				½ mark
Software licence T0 = $3k x 16 users T1 - 2 = $3k x 8 users	(48.0)	(24.0)	(24.0)		1 mark
Training T0 = 16 users x $0.5K T1 - 2 = 8 users x $0.25k	(8.0)	(2.0)	(2.0)		1 mark
Net cashflow	(321.0)	112.0	137.0	163.0	
Discount factor 6%	1.000	0.943	0.890	0.840	
Present value	(321.0)	105.6	121.9	136.9	
Net Present Value	**43.5**				1 mark

The new system has a positive NPV, which indicates that it would be an appropriate project to undertake from a purely financial perspective. However, there are significant issues surrounding the figures that need to be addressed.

The project generates its positive cash flows from saved staff costs and recovered margin on previously lost sales. Both of these figures need to be validated.

<u>Recovered margin</u>
The figure appears very approximate, in that it is quoted as a percentage of total sales. More robust analysis needs to be conducted to validate whether this applies more to a particular product and therefore whether the 14% margin is a realistic figure. Furthermore, the assumption that revenue and margins will remain constant for three years is too simplistic for a serious project such as this.

<u>Saved staff costs</u>
The Operations Director has not been consulted on whether the savings are realistic. Bearing in mind that he is the one who will need to manage operations, his opinion on staffing levels is important. Furthermore, the costs of redundancy have been omitted from the calculation. With five positions being made redundant, it is entirely possible that this could make the project unviable, as suggested by the HR Director.

The IT Director, by his own admission, has not investigated alternatives to MNO as a supplier. Given that MNO is due to receive SK$358k from this arrangement, the IT Director should put the project out to tender. This will either validate MNO's offer as realistic or identify other providers who could do the same work for a lower price. Whatever the outcome, these costs should not be accepted without question.

It appears that the IT Director has only budgeted for licenses for Operations staff. Depending on how the system is being used, it is entirely possible that other users (eg finance staff) will require access for data analysis purposes.

It is recommended that the new IT system is implemented. It generates a positive discounted cash flow of SK$43.5k over three years and addresses some serious shortfalls in V's processes that will increasingly undermine its competitive position (eg lost revenue due to cancelled holidays). However, the project does require the involvement of all the directors to ensure that the savings are accurately calculated. Furthermore, it would be appropriate to put out a tender for the work as there may be other suppliers able to do the same job at a more competitive rate.

Question 2

Marking scheme

	Marks

Requirement (a)

Explanation of Porter's generic strategies (1 mark each)

Cost leadership, differentiation, focus, stuck in the middle — **4**

Identification of existing products in strategies (1 mark each) — **3**

Advice (1 – 2 marks per well developed point)
Ideas could include:
No consistency across brand
Need more info on package holidays
No crossover between products due to confusion
Consistent brand would allow natural development through family life cycle
Establish core message (e.g. quality service regardless of standard of hotel rooms) — <u>Max 5</u>
MAXIMUM FOR REQUIREMENT — <u>**12**</u>

Requirement (b)

Calculations
<u>Care Holidays</u>
Total revenue — 1
Commission payable to V — 1
Lost margin — 1
Total training — 1
Calculation of NPV — 1

<u>Conference</u>
Total revenue from room hire — 1
Total catering costs — 1
Mark-up on catering costs — 1
Net income — 1
Calculation of Expected Value — 1

Analysis
<u>Care Holidays</u> (1 – 2 marks per well developed point to a maximum of 3)
Payback not achieved until Year 4 (Yr 5 if using discounted payback)
Indicates high risk venture
Reliant on revenue figures from provider (need validation)
Query whether 10% is appropriate cost of capital, given level of risk — Max 3

<u>Conference</u> (1 – 2 marks per well developed point to a maximum of 2)
Positive EV, but only due to high value of best outcome
Only 15% probability of making a gain on project — <u>Max 2</u>
MAXIMUM FOR REQUIREMENT — <u>**15**</u>

Requirement (c)

<u>Ansoff's Matrix</u>
Evaluation of each opportunity **using Ansoff's matrix**
<u>Product development</u> (new product, existing market)
Care Holidays   1
Evaluation of opportunity (1 – 2 marks per well developed point to a maximum of 4)
    Make use of existing brand loyalty
    Makes use of a gap in the market to access a demographic previously un-catered for
    May be too niche / expensive for customer base
    May not be an attractive product   Max 4

<u>Market development</u> (existing product, new market)
Corporate bookings   1
Evaluation of opportunity (1 – 2 marks per well developed point to a maximum of 3)
    Maintain proven product range (v. popular with customers)
    Expand into demographic not previously attracted – increase market share
    Existing product may not be exciting enough to attract new customers
    Damage to brand if discounts are associated with it (creates expectations)   Max 4

<u>Diversification</u> (new product, new market)
Conferences   1
Evaluation of opportunity (1 – 2 marks per well developed point to a maximum of 4)
    Highest risk as new product and market
    Heavy reliance on providers (conference centre & caterers)
    Their performance will impact on V brand   <u>Max 4</u>
MAXIMUM FOR REQUIREMENT   **<u>15</u>**

Requirement (d)

1 mark for identifying an ethical issue; 1 mark for relating it to the CIMA code of ethics

<u>Care holidays</u>
"Assertive" selling is inappropriate given the target customer – breach of professional behaviour   2
Under-qualified staff – breach of professional competence and due care   2

<u>Conferences</u>
Catering contract to a friend – breach of objectivity (no experience of the industry)   2

<u>Corporate bookings</u>
Misleading staff into believing they're receiving a special discount – breach of integrity   2
Access to staff records – breach of confidentiality   <u>2</u>
MAXIMUM FOR REQUIREMENT   **<u>MAX 8</u>**

TOTAL FOR QUESTION   **<u>50</u>**

Suggested solution

(a)   Michael Porter identifies three generic strategies that can generate competitive advantage:

Cost leadership
Porter describes businesses that pride themselves on being the lowest cost producer as being cost leaders. Families with young children seeking a package holiday are likely to be price sensitive. The number of family members makes price a more sensitive issue, and the attraction of a pre-packaged holiday is often seen as a low-risk and relatively low cost solution. V's package holidays are described as "cut-price holiday deals" which means that they are likely to be cost leaders.

[Tutorial note: A "cut-price" selling price does not inevitably link to low cost production. Credit is available to students who give reasonable justifications for classifying package holidays differently.]

Differentiation
Companies which offer something of value that their competitors don't are referred to as "differentiators". V's Prestige Travel differentiates itself by only offering "upmarket" hotels. Unlike the Adventure holidays, customers pay a considerable premium for luxury.

Focus
Porter explains that some companies restrict their activities to one particular segment (or niche) of a market and then compete on a cost leadership or differentiation basis. These niches tend to be very specific – in the case of V, this might involve specialising in luxury hotels in one location.

The Adventure holidays offered by V are good examples of cost leadership focus. They are designed to appeal to travellers with very limited funds who are prepared to accept low standards of accommodation ("back-packing") when travelling.

Having a portfolio of products that contains both cost leaders and differentiators can cause problems for an organisation such as V.

Stuck in the middle
Porter warns that, when a company is unclear about which strategy it is following, it risks becoming "stuck in the middle". This is when the company offers a product or service that has expensive components (ie not a cost leader) but ones that a customer is not prepared to pay extra for (ie does not differentiate).

In V's case, by being both a cost leader and a differentiator, it risks confusing its customers and being stuck in the middle. So, Adventure customers may no longer want to rough it if they have a young family, so would be likely to assume that V would be unable to help them. Similarly, customers who have used V for Prestige travel would be unlikely to recommend the company to grown-up children who are looking to go back-packing. ITD's comments that customers are not transferring from one product to another bears out this theory.

Action
V needs to send a clear message to customers as to its offering. This can be achieved by developing sub-brands for each product that are underpinned by the overall "V" brand. This would allow the three products to develop their own unique marketing message (whether cost leader, differentiator or focus) while retaining affiliation to an overall concept.

In the case of V, its overall brand is likely to be based on customer service. The message of treating customers properly is entirely compatible with each of Porter's generic strategies. This has been done effectively by supermarkets such as Sainsbury's that offer a premium , standard and cost-leadership food ranges under the same brand.

BPP
LEARNING MEDIA

(b)

Care Holidays

	T0	T1	T2	T3	T4	T5	
Number of customer nights		5,000	6,000	7,000	8,000	9,000	
	$	$	$	$	$	$	
Total revenue ($2.5k / customer night)		12,500,000	15,000,000	17,500,000	20,000,000	22,500,000	1 mark
V's commission (5% revenue)		625,000	750,000	875,000	1,000,000	1,125,000	1 mark
Less: lost margin (27.5% revenue x 15% margin)		(515,625)	(618,750)	(721,875)	(825,000)	(928,125)	1 mark
Training ($2.5k x 2 staff x 50 branches)	(500,000)						1 mark
Net cash flow	(500,000)	109,375	131,250	153,125	175,000	196,875	
Discount Factor (10%)	1	0.909	0.826	0.751	0.683	0.621	
Present Value	(500,000)	99,422	108,413	114,997	119,525	122,259	
Net Present Value	**64,616**						1 mark

Conferences

	Worst	Likely	Best	TOTAL	
No. bookings received	15	20	30		
	$	$	$	$	
Daily charge for room hire	35,000	29,000	27,000		
Total revenue from room hire	525,000	580,000	810,000		1 mark
Catering (per booking)	90,000	120,000	160,000		
Total catering	1,350,000	2,400,000	4,800,000		1 mark
Mark up of 15%	176,087	313,043	626,087		1 mark
Total income	701,087	893,043	1,436,087		
Less venue hire ($30,000 x 30 days)	(900,000)	(900,000)	(900,000)		
Net cash flow	(198,913)	(6,957)	536,087		1 mark
Probability	35%	50%	15%		
Expected Value (net cash flow x probability)	(69,620)	(3,478)	80,413	**7,315**	1 mark

<u>Care holidays</u>
This project has a positive NPV of SK$65k. However, there are a number of concerns with these figures:

- The figures are reliant on sales estimates from T who have a vested interest in V selling their products. The objectivity of these figures needs to be confirmed, especially given the ambitious growth forecast.

- Even using these figures, payback is not achieved until Year 4 (Year 5 using discounted payback). Given that this only a five year contract, this indicates a high level of risk.

- The 10% cost of capital figure is used by V for all projects. It would be appropriate, under the circumstances, to use a higher cost of capital to reflect the risk of offering a new and untested product.

<u>Conference</u>
This project has an expected value of SK$7,315. However, as with the care holidays, there are concerns with this figure:

- The figure is not directly comparable to the care holidays, as it shows an annual return, while the care holidays represent a five year contract.

- There is an 85% probability that the project will operate at a loss in any given year (worst / most likely outcomes both show negative cash flows).

Given that this project will only be repeated annually, it is unlikely that there will be sufficient repetition to make the expected value meaningful.

To conclude, while both projects show positive cash flows, neither of them are as attractive as ITD suggests. More careful investigation needs to be conducted before committing to either of them.

(c)   <u>Care holidays</u>
        This involves presenting a new product to an existing customer base and therefore corresponds to <u>product development</u> on Ansoff's matrix.

        V has the potential to make use of its brand and good standing with its current customers to launch this new product. It also has the potential to attract new customers, thus increasing its overall market share.

        However, this product caters for a very narrow market segment, namely housebound people and their carers with a very high disposable income. It is possible that the level of investment required (specifically in the time and cost of training) may not justify the return generated.

        Finally, there is no guarantee that V's Prestige customers will take to this idea. The whole issue of "home help" care is a highly sensitive area and the prospect of going away to a hotel will not be attractive to all people in this position.

        <u>Corporate bookings</u>
        By marketing its existing product range to a new geographical segment, this project would be seen in Ansoff's matrix as <u>market development</u>.

        V's existing customers seem to like the products. Although there is some difficulty retaining them when their needs change, there is no indication that there are any concerns about the holidays themselves. It therefore makes sense to offer these reliable products to new customers. This has the potential to increase market share.

        However, the products themselves may not be exciting enough to generate a significant increase in market share. It may be that the staff at ABC do not fall into the "young family" demographic that the package holidays caters for.

BPP
LEARNING MEDIA

Furthermore, the staff at ABC are not being offered anything that cannot be purchased online by any member of the public. There is a risk that V's reputation will be damaged if and when staff realise that the apparently special offers are nothing of the kind.

Conferences
This provision of a new service to a new type of customer would be classified as diversification on Ansoff's matrix.

Diversification has the potential for the highest returns, as it expands into new markets and products that are not currently being exploited by V. Given the limited availability of suitable venues, this could become a highly lucrative expansion.

However, with high potential return comes high risk. V's brand will be impacted by the performance of A-Centre and the caterer – if either of them fail to meet the required standards, V's reputation will be damaged and this could impact on other operations.

Furthermore, V has to invest $900,000 in room bookings which it may not be able to sell on. The opportunity to enter into some sort of agency or licensing agreement with A-Centre might be explored so that the risk can be, to some extent, mitigated.

(d)   The CIMA Code of Ethics has five dimensions:

Professional behaviour
The "assertive" sales course being offered to staff selling T's holidays is unethical. There needs to be recognition that the target customer is likely to be a vulnerable person who could be taken advantage of, particularly if sales targets and bonuses are involved. T's holidays seem popular enough without having to adopt an assertive (not to say aggressive) approach. V should ensure that any training focuses on treating the customer with sensitivity and dignity.

Professional competence and due care
The comments from T's marketing director indicate that not all of T's customers will receive care from people with the required qualifications. Given the serious need for proper "home help" support and the expectation created by the premium location and price, this is a breach of the level of care guests will reasonably expect. It is not acceptable for T to expect unqualified staff to take care of guests' "home help" needs. As well as being unethical, this could have legal implications if a guest was injured as a result of a lack of care by an unqualified assistant. V needs assurance that all of T's customers will receive the required level of care.

Objectivity
In proposing that his friend is used to cater for conferences, IT has failed to show objectivity. While there is no suggestion that his friend is dishonest, the fact that he has only just started out in this industry indicates that there may be concerns over his ability to deliver the scale of catering required (5,000 people). Other caterers should be investigated via a formal tendering process and the final decision made based on their ability to meet the customer needs rather than any personal history.

Integrity
Staff at ABC are being misled into thinking they are being given a "unique promotion" when they are not. Quite apart from the damage to V's reputation that will arise when staff discover this, it is unethical of V to allow its products to be presented in this misleading manner.

Confidentiality
In giving access to staff records, ABC is breaching its duty of confidentiality to its staff. V should not accept or use this information unless staff have consented to being contacted in this way.

Question 3

Marking scheme

	Marks
Requirement (a)	
Brief explanation of the value chain	1
Benefits that V might gain from applying the value chain – Up to 2 marks for each benefit explained	Up to 12
Limitations of applying the value chain to V – Up to 2 marks for each limitation explained	<u>Up to 4</u>
MAXIMUM FOR REQUIREMENT	**14**
Requirement (b) (i)	
Calculation of revenue – ½ mark for each product type	Up to 2
Calculation of margin – ½ mark for each product type	Up to 2
Calculation of costs – ½ mark for each cost; and calculation of contribution to profit - ½ mark	<u>Up to 2</u>
MAXIMUM FOR REQUIREMENT	<u>**6**</u>
Requirement (b) (ii)	
Evaluation of relevant advantages of closing all the branches (if any identified) – Up to 2	2
Evaluation of disadvantages of closing all the branches – Up to 2 marks each	Up to 6
Evaluation of relevant advantages of closing some of the branches – Up to 2 marks each	Up to 4
Evaluation of disadvantages of closing only some of the branches – Up to 2 marks each	<u>Up to 4</u>
Note: Credit is not to be given twice if the same advantage or disadvantage is attributed to closing both all and some of the branches	
MAXIMUM FOR REQUIREMENT	<u>**10**</u>
Requirement (c)	
For each benefit of using environmental analysis to help decide whether or not to close the branches advised – Up to 2 marks each (1 mark for identifying a relevant benefit; 1 mark applying it to the decision to close the shops).	<u>Up to 8</u>
Any generic benefits of environmental analysis, not embedded in the scenario, to be capped at 1 mark each	
MAXIMUM FOR REQUIREMENT	<u>**8**</u>
Requirement (d)	
Identification the importance of stakeholder analysis in relation to managing the closures – 1 mark	1
For each issue to be considered in relation to implementing the closures – Up to 2 marks each	Up to 6
For each relevant way of overcoming resistance to change – Up to 2 marks each	
(Note: No marks are to be given for generic discussions of force field analysis or Kotter & Schlesinger's methods of overcoming resistance to change)	<u>Up to 8</u>
MAXIMUM FOR REQUIREMENT	<u>**12**</u>
TOTAL FOR QUESTION	<u>**50**</u>

Suggested solution

(a)

Identify sources of value - The value chain illustrates the way in which business activities link together to add value from the customer's perspective.

Benefits

Personal service - If V conducted a value chain analysis, this would force it to identify how it creates value for their customers. It appears that the main source of value is enabling customers to discuss holiday alternatives with staff, to find the holiday which best suits their requirements.

However, as a number of potential customers appear to be researching their holidays themselves, V could use the ideas of the value chain to identify whether there are some types of holiday for which it can to add value more effectively than others. In this case, it appears that V is most able to continue to add value for Prestige holidays, which might suggest that V is better to tailor its business to Prestige holidays going forward, rather than offering a broader range of Package or Adventure holidays. In this way, V will be able to maximise the competitive advantage it can get from one of its key competences – the friendly direct personal service that it offers customers.

Identify competitive advantage and generic strategy - In this respect, the value chain could also be used to complement Porter's generic strategies. V's major differentiating factor (direct personal service) is becoming less important for people booking Package or Adventure holidays. However, it appears still to be important for people booking Prestige holidays. Therefore, it might seem sensible for V to pursue a focussed differentiation strategy, based around Prestige holidays and high quality customer service, rather than trying to offer all three different kinds of holiday products.

Nonetheless, value chain analysis might still lead V to question how far its competitive advantage is sustainable. In particular, as the number of customers researching and booking their own holidays increases, V should be asking itself what value it can offer its customers that they could not generate for themselves? If V is not able to offer its customers some kind of value-adding services in the longer term, then ultimately its business will not be sustainable.

Customer representatives – The 'service' activity in the value chain will also highlight the potential importance of the customer representative at holiday destinations to provide support to V's customers. It is likely that these representatives are most valuable for package holidays; and so if V changes its product mix it will need to consider what impact this has on the way it uses customer representatives. For example, if it increases the number of bespoke destinations it serves under Prestige Travel holidays, would V still be able to guarantee that its customers get the standard of holiday and level of service they expect?

Cost drivers – As well as identifying sources of value, the value chain also illustrates how costs are caused in a business. One of the key benefits of the value chain for V could come from encouraging it to look at the relationship between the value being added and the costs being incurred in its business activities.

In particular, as price is becoming an increasingly important issue for potential customers (particularly in relation to Package or Adventure holidays) V could use the idea of the value chain to identify whether any of its current activities do not add value for customers. If this is the case, these activities should either be discontinued or done more cheaply.

Firm infrastructure – The net operating profit margins for V's branches are lower than those for its online business due to the operating and administration costs in the branches. Analysis of its firm infrastructure may help V identify some areas of cost saving in its branches, possibly even extending as far as closing some (or all) of the branches if the overheads are too high compared to the amount of revenue they generate.

However, V could also question whether the staff dealing with online enquiries and bookings need to be based at its head office in SK's capital city. For example, operating costs such as wages or rates may be higher there than in some other parts of the country. Therefore, V might be able to make savings by relocating the staff dealing with enquiries and bookings.

Marketing – The majority of V's marketing comes from the literature it produces about the holiday products it sells. Here again, the value chain might encourage V to question the relationship between costs and value. It seems likely that the majority of V's marketing expenditure will be for printed brochures for its shops. However, what is the correlation between people looking at V's marketing literature and then buying a holiday in the shop?

Human resource management – There appear to be no succession plans in place for when the Executive Chairman retires in June 2013. Given that he is also the majority shareholder, it would seem likely that the Chairman retiring could have a significant impact on the business, and therefore – if they have not already done so already – the remaining directors should start thinking about how to deal with this.

Limitations

Service business – The value chain was designed for use with manufacturing businesses, and it cannot always be easily applied to service organisations.

V's key capability is likely to be the knowledge of its sales consultants, who use this knowledge to design holiday packages in response to the demands of their clients.

In this respect, understanding customer requirements and designing solutions which fulfil them is likely to be a critical business process for V; however, it does not fit nearly into any of the primary activities in the value chain (which are more suitable for dealing with tangible inputs and outputs).

Conversely, although 'outbound logistics' is considered one of the primary activities in Porter's value chain it does not appear to be a major issue for V.

> Tutorial note: It is debatable how 'inbound logistics' would apply to V. V needs to buy up different types of holiday from different providers for the times required by its customers, and secure suitable flights, in order for customers to book them. We might treat these activities as 'inbound logistics' or else they could be seen as 'procurement.'
>
> Again, ideas of value could be useful here; in particular, around the extent to which V is able to source holidays which individual customers couldn't find so easily themselves.

(b)

(i)

Impact of branch closures

	Package	Adventure	Prestige	Support	Total
Revenue					
Total (SK $)	90	60	95	5	250
High street %	20%	21%	70%	60%	
High street (SK $)	18	12.6	66.5	3	100.1
Margin					
	30%	25%	45%	30%	
Margin (SK $)	5.40	3.15	29.93	0.90	**39.38**

Less share of operating and admin costs	
Staff costs (75%)	12.38
Marketing (80%)	8.80
Other operating costs(70%)	10.15
Contribution to profit – per year	**8.05**

(ii)

Contribution to profit – The calculations show that if V closes all of its high street branches, this will lead to a reduction in contribution to profit of SK $8.05 million per year; which represents a reduction of 23% in V's operating profit.

Given that one of V's financial objectives is to grow earnings by an average of 5% per year, the decision to close all the branches is unlikely to be appropriate, unless any additional online earnings will be greater than them amount lost.

It may be that branch revenues would fall in future anyway, but we do not have any forecast figures to 2012-2013 so we can only compare the loss of revenue against the actual results for 2012.

Return on investment – It seems likely that V has invested a large amount of capital in its shops, so it should also look at their profitability in relation to the amount of capital invested. In particular, if V could generate a better return on its capital (for example, through investing in IT and expanding its online services) then this could justify the decision to close the shops.

Prestige travel revenue – However, if V closes all its high street branches, it could potentially lose 70% of its prestige travel bookings, because the customers who book these high value bespoke holidays prefer to do so in person rather than online.

Currently Prestige travel is the largest contributor to V's total revenue, and, importantly, V also earns a higher margin on Prestige products than on other products. Therefore, V should be looking to retain as many of its 'Prestige' customers as possible.

In this respect, V could consider whether it could offer a telephone booking service for customers who would prefer to speak to an agent, rather than booking their holidays online.

Product profitability – The Finance Director's point about product profitability could be important here. It seems likely that 'Prestige' travel holidays are much more profitable for V than either Package or Adventure holidays.

Therefore, if there are some branches which sell a high proportion of Prestige holidays, they are likely to be profitable, and so it would not seem sensible for V to close them. However, if there are other branches which sell mainly Package or Adventure holidays, these are likely to be less profitable and so it might be more appropriate to close them. In this case, the alternative proposal may be more appropriate than the original proposal to close all the shops; although the revised proposal still seems to contradict an objective of growing earnings year on year.

Customer demographics – Although the total number of bookings in V's high street shops has fallen in recent years, the number of Prestige holidays has remained largely constant. This again suggests that the customers who buy Prestige holidays are a valuable market segment for V, particularly as they appear to be content to continue buying their holidays in person from a travel agent, rather than switching to designing them themselves online.

In this respect, V may find that its high street branches are better placed to sustain a niche business providing 'Prestige' holidays than its online business – which again suggests V retain at least some of its branches.

Sustainability of online business – The trend for people to 'build' their own holidays suggests that, in future, fewer people overall will use V or other agencies, either online or on the high street.

In this case, if V closes its high street shops, with their core of 'Prestige' holiday-makers, it will become even more vulnerable to a shift among Package and Adventure holiday-makers towards building their own holidays.

Based on the figures to the end of June 2012, just under 80% of V's online revenue comes from Package and Adventure holiday-makers (see Working). However, these are the groups which are most likely to stop using travel agencies in favour of building their own holidays.

Therefore this suggests that the decision to close the high street branches would make V more vulnerable to the trend towards disintermediation in the holiday buying market.

Economies of scale – One of the dangers of closing some, but not all, of V's shops is that it could lose economies of scale. For example, it may be able to negotiate favourable unit prices on its promotional literature on account of the volumes it buys. In this case, the decision to reduce the number of shops could have a slight negative impact on the profitability of the remaining shops.

Equally, it is not clear what overheads relate to the high street branches as a whole. Again, if V has to apportion central overheads over a lower number of branch units, this could reduce the net profitability of the remaining shops.

Negative publicity – If V decides to close some, but not all, of its branches, this could generate negative publicity. In particular, customers at the remaining branches may be concerned that their branch is also going to close shortly, and so may look for alternative travel agents to buy their holiday through.

Working:

Online revenues:

Package: 80% of SK $90m = SK $72m

Adventure: 79% of SK $60m = SK $47.4m

Prestige: 30% of SK $95m = SK $28.5m

Support: 40% of SK $5m = SK $2m

Proportion of revenue from Package & Adventure: SK $119.4m / $150m = 79.6%.

(c)

> **Tutorial note:** In part (a) we looked at the potential benefit of looking at V's internal resources and its value chain in strategic planning. Here we now look at the importance of external factors.
>
> An additional point you could highlight (which we haven't made in the answer below) is the importance of considering both external and internal factors before making any decision about possible branch closures.

Understanding the company's strategic environment – The Executive Chairman seems convinced that customer service and customer satisfaction alone will be sufficient for V's continuing success.

However, the recent newspaper report suggested that other factors – notably price – are crucial in customers' decisions about which holidays to buy. This may indicate that the Chairman no longer understands V's market as well as he could. However, it is important that V does have a good understanding of the market in which it operates, before making any strategic decision – such as a decision to close its branches.

Strategic planning – It appears that V does not place much emphasis on strategic planning, and, until five years ago, the board had never engaged in long-term planning. However, given the importance of any potential decision to close its branches, it is important that V considers as many relevant factors as possible before making the decision. For example, it would be useful to identify all the major stakeholders who would be interested in the decision, and consider either how they could affect the decision or how they could be affected by it.

Equally it will be important for V to identify the trends and environmental factors (PEST factors) affecting the industry, and then to assess how B should respond to them. For example, if the environmental factors reinforce the idea that V's online business is vulnerable to consumers building their own holidays, this would suggest that V should not close its branches in the short term whilst it tries to develop an alternative business model.

Understanding the customers – One particularly important aspect of V's environment to understand will be its customers. We have already suggested that, in general terms, 'Prestige' customers seem to be more committed to continue using V's branches than other broad customer groups. However, it could be useful for V to have

BPP
LEARNING MEDIA

some more detailed market segmentation of its customers to see if there any other patterns which could help predict usage and future profitability of its shops.

Equally, having a better understanding of its customers may help V assess whether some branches are likely to remain more profitable than others, which in turn might suggest that it should keep some of its branches open rather than closing them all.

Identify threats – However, the newspaper report also shows that the market is changing rapidly, and a number of the changes present threats to V; in particular, the increase in the number of people choosing to design their own holidays.

In this respect, environmental analysis could help V understand the threats to profitability in the travel industry as whole. In effect, the way consumers are using technology to book their own holidays, has created a substitute service to the travel business which V provides.

V then needs to consider how any decision to close the shops could help it deal with the threats if faces, or else build on any new opportunities which arise in the industry.

(d)

Stakeholders – The directors need to consider the context of the change, and this can be done by looking at the stakeholders who will be affected by it. Their resistance to the change could have a significant impact on V's ability to implement the changes as smoothly as it might want to.

In this case, the most important groups of stakeholders for V to consider are employees and customers; they both have a high degree of interest in the decision but a relatively low level of power. Therefore, it will be important for V to inform both groups about the changes, and to explain the reasons for them.

Staff

It is inevitable that the branch staff will not support the change, because it is their jobs being made redundant. However, it is important that V tries to maintain as constructive a relationship with the staff as possible between the closures being announced and the shops actually shutting; for example, so that they continue to provide high levels of customer service to any customers who want to book holidays in that period.

Motivating staff during the change period

Possible alternative employment within V – If there are any vacancies at any other branches near those being closed, staff at risk of losing their jobs should be given the opportunity of applying for the vacancies.

Redundancy terms – The staff should be offered redundancies packages which are more generous than the statutory minimum, but these enhanced packages will be dependent on the staff continuing to offer high quality service during their notice period.

Alternative employment outside V – Similarly, the staff should be offered help finding alternative employment (for example, by V arranging interview training and CV writing for them); but again, these packages should be linked to them continuing to maintain a high standard of work during their notice period.

Customers

Again, it seems unlikely that customers affected will support the change, if it means that their local branch of V is closing.

However, it is important that V handles the change as sensitively as possible so that it can retain as many of the customers as it can; either because they will use the larger branch nearby, or because they will book through V's online travel booking service.

Customer retention – In this respect, V might consider contacting all the customers who had booked holidays within the last year at the branches which are closing, notifying them of the closure, but also offering them a discount if they book their next holiday with V.

Customer support – It is important that V communicates to customers who have booked holidays through the branches but not yet been on their holidays to reassure them that V as a whole continues to operate, and so the service provided by the customer representatives on their holidays will not be affected by the branch closures.

Other stakeholders which could be relevant:

> **Local press** – V could consider notifying the local press in the five locations, so that the public are informed about the branch closures but also reassured that V's other branches remain open, and will still continue to provide the high levels of customer service which customers have come to expect from V.
>
> **Suppliers** – V should notify any suppliers which deal directly with the branches in question that those branches will be closing. It should also adjust any more general orders and deliveries (such as marketing brochures) to reflect the reduction in branch numbers from 50 to 45. However, perhaps more importantly, V needs to ensure holiday and flight providers that it is still operating overall.

Time constraints – Another important factor the directors to consider is the timetable for any changes. The change is a one-off, discontinuous change, and so could potentially be made quite quickly. However, the directors should consider what impression a rapid closure will give to customers and staff. In this respect, they may prefer to set the closures further in advance, making it clear that these are planned changes.

Cost – V should also consider any costs associated with the closures. The most obvious ones are redundancy payments. As turnover of staff is relatively low, some of the staff may have worked for V for a long time in which case they could be entitled to quite large redundancy payments.

However, alongside redundancy payments, V should also consider whether it has any leases, for example, which it will have to continue to pay even if it closes the branch. In turn, this analysis of costs and payments could influence the timescale V chooses for the closure of the branches.

Question 4

Marking scheme

	Marks

Requirement (a)

Evaluation of the advantages of measuring non-financial aspects of performance – Up to 2 marks for each advantage evaluated — Up to 6

Evaluation of the potential limitations of measuring non-financial aspects of performance – Up to 2 marks for each limitation evaluated — Up to 4

For overall comment on the benefit of measuring both financial and non-financial aspects of performance – Up to 2 marks — Up to 2

MAXIMUM FOR REQUIREMENT — **8**

Requirement (b)

Each perspective of the Scorecard explained – Up to 1 mark each — Up to 4

MAXIMUM FOR REQUIREMENT — **4**

Requirement (c) (i)

For each relevant advantage of introducing the Scorecard at V, well explained and related to the scenario – Up to 2 marks each — Up to 6

For any generic relevant advantages of introducing the Scorecard in general terms, not related to the scenario – max ½ mark each

MAXIMUM FOR REQUIREMENT — **6**

Requirement (c) (ii)

For each problem related to introducing the Scorecard at V; well explained and related to the scenario – Up to 2 marks each — Up to 6

For any generic problems related to introducing the Scorecard, but not related to the scenario – max ½ mark each

MAXIMUM FOR REQUIREMENT — **6**

Requirement (d)

For calculating the commission receivable from HN under the Exclusive deal – Up to 4 marks — Up to 4

For calculating the total commissions receivable from HN and TL under the non-Exclusive deals – Up to 5 marks — Up to 5

For discussions of relevant issues which should influence the decision whether or not to accept the Exclusive deal – Up to 3 marks for each relevant issue. — Up to 9

Clear recommendation about whether or not to accept the deal; consistent with discussion of issues – Up to 2 marks — Up to 2

MAXIMUM FOR REQUIREMENT — **18**

Requirement (e)

For brief discussion of corporate social responsibility – 1 mark — 1

For discussion of corporate social responsibility issues; well explained and related to the scenario – Up to 2 marks each — Up to 8

MAXIMUM FOR REQUIREMENT — **8**

TOTAL FOR QUESTION — **50**

Suggested solution

(a)

Importance of non-financial measures – Customer satisfaction and increasing product range and choice have both been identified as being potentially critical success factors for V. By performing well in these areas of the business, V should be better placed to sustain its financial performance than if it performs badly in them. For example, if V is able to achieve a high level of customer retention, as a result of keeping its customers satisfied, this should help it maintain its revenues.

In this case, there would seem to be a clear link between non-financial performance and financial performance.

However, the directors are not currently monitoring how well V is performing in non-financial aspects of this business. As a result they may not notice performance issues which subsequently have an impact on V's financial results.

Strategic goals – In many companies, the non-financial performance measures which get monitored are linked to the company's strategic goals and objectives. However, V does not currently appear to have identified what its strategic goals and objectives are. (It has only identified some high level financial objectives). In this respect, having an increased focus on non-financial aspects of performance might also encourage the Directors to think about what the company's strategic objectives should be.

Additionally, if the Directors monitor the non-financial aspects of performance this might also help them be able to identify objectives and provide incentives for branch managers and other the managers of the online business, designed to help them improve operational performance.

Forecasting and predictions – Another potential benefit of looking at non-financial performance indicators is that they could help V forecast its future performance more accurately. Again, for example, if it becomes clear that customer retention rates are falling, this could alert the Directors that revenue and profits are also likely to start falling in future (unless they take action to reverse the decline in performance).

In this respect, monitoring financial performance helps the Directors analyse past performance, but monitoring aspects of non-financial performance could be more useful for looking forwards.

However, it is important that the Directors continue to monitor financial performance alongside non-financial performance, because there is no guarantee that favourable non-financial performance will necessarily translate into favourable financial performance. For example, even though V may score very highly in customer service feedback, V's revenues might still fall if customers find they can buy holidays more cheaply by dealing directly with hotel operators rather than using an intermediary such as V.

Linkages – The directors also need to be careful which non-financial measures they choose to monitor, and in particular how the non-financial measures link to V's financial performance. For example, there will be little value in measuring aspects of operational performance which add little value to V's financial performance.

In this respect, it is also important that the Directors continue to monitor financial performance as well as financial performance. As the Directors are also V's shareholders, the ultimate measure of performance will be how well V is generating financial value (through profits and dividends) for them.

As the Executive Chairman and the Finance Director have both indicated, V is operating in tough trading conditions. This reinforces the need to continue to monitor aspects of V's financial performance; for example, to see whether sales are increasing or decreasing in a competitive market, and how well V is controlling its costs.

(b)

(i)

The balanced scorecard aims to highlight the **financial and non-financial elements** of corporate performance, through measuring **four perspectives of performance**: financial, customer satisfaction, internal efficiency and innovation.

Financial perspective – This addresses the question, 'How can we succeed financially and create value for our owners?' (which in V's case is the Directors.) It covers measures such as growth, profitability, liquidity and return on capital employed.

Customer perspective – This considers how an organisation must appear to its customers in order to be successful. It asks the question 'What do new and existing customers expect of us?' – aspects which could be measured in terms of quality, reliability and value for money of the organisation's products.

Internal business perspective – This considers what business processes an organisation needs to excel at in order to achieve financial and customer objectives. For example, it could be measured in relation to the speed and efficiency of an online booking process.

Innovation and learning perspective – This considers how an organisation can continue to create value and maintain its competitive position through improvement and change. It could be measured, for example, in relation to the acquisition of new skills, or the development of new products.

(c) (i)

Determine objectives and measures – The balanced scorecard seeks to provide a link between an organisation's strategy and its operational performance. Currently, V does not seem to have a mission statement or any formal strategic objectives and so it will need to develop these in order to determine what performance measures should be included in the scorecard.

It seems that the Directors have already begun to identify some of the factors which they believe will be critical to its success (excellent customer service; having an extensive product range) and introducing the scorecard should encourage them to develop performance measures linked to these critical success factors.

Range of perspectives – The balanced scorecard looks at a range of perspectives rather than only financial ones. In this way, introducing the scorecard will reinforce the importance of measuring financial and non-financial aspects of performance.

For example, the innovation and learning perspective of the scorecard could highlight the importance of staff training, in relation to giving staff the knowledge they need to support an increased product range. However, the Scorecard could also encourage a greater focus on the way V uses the intranet to share knowledge, and how information is shared among customer-facing staff more generally.

Internal and external factors – The balanced scorecard will encourage the Directors to look at both internal and external factors of performance. The tough trading conditions are making V's environment increasingly competitive, so V will need to work harder to attract and retain customers, and may need to find new and innovative ways of doing so. The 'Customer' perspective of the Scorecard highlights the importance of meeting customer expectations, while the 'Innovation' perspective also highlights the importance of trying to identifying new ways to offer value to the customer.

However, the Scorecard also highlights the importance of V's internal business processes being as efficient as possible – both so that it can serve its customers as well as possible, and also so that it can generate as much profit as possible.

Identify linkages – The process of implementing the Balanced Scorecard will also encourage V to think about the linkages between the four perspectives; in particular, how the companies performance in non-financial matters links to its financial performance. In this respect, introducing the Scorecard could help redress the focus of management's attention, and prevent them becoming too narrowly focused on financial aspects of performance alone.

(c) (ii)

Selecting measures – It seems unlikely that any of the Directors or staff within V have any previous experience of using the Scorecard or any similar performance frameworks. Therefore, they could have difficulties selecting the most appropriate measures to use, or even deciding how many measures to include in their Scorecard.

Although the Directors have realised the importance of monitoring non-financial aspects of performance alongside the financial aspects they currently monitor, it is important they do not select too many measures to include in the Scorecard. If V selects too many measures, this could lead to information overload, and the risk that key pieces of information get hidden by other information.

In this respect, it is important that V selects measures which relate to key processes or key success factors which will help V achieve its strategic aims. However, this could be problematic if V hasn't decided what its key strategic aims and objectives are.

Conflicting measures – For the Scorecard to help improve V's performance, the measures chosen need to be congruent. However, this may not always be the case, and some measures may be conflicting. For example, V may select a measure looking at the number of new products it introduces. However, if it increases its product range too much such that customer-facing staff are not aware of the details properly, the quality of service they offer customers might fall, which in turn could also affect customer retention rates.

Capturing information

Once V has decided which performance measures to include in the Scorecard and has set performance targets for them, it will need to capture the necessary information to see how well it is performing against those targets. Although it appears that the management information systems relating to V's branches provide reasonably detailed information, it is not clear whether V has similar management information for its online business.

Equally, it is not clear how V will capture any information it may require in relation to the number of new products introduced, or the level of training and staff development offered.

Possible additional point:

Staff not understanding the need for the scorecard

Given that V is already profitable under the current control and performance measurement system, staff many not understand why a new, seemingly more complex performance measurement system has to be introduced. In this case, they may resist the introduction of the scorecard, particularly if they feel that linking their performance to a wider range of indicators will make it harder for them to achieve their bonuses, or if they feel that they will have to spend more time recording different aspects of their performance rather than getting on with their jobs in the ways they are used to.

(d)

Calculation of commissions earned

	Year 1	Year 2	Year 3	Year 4	Year 5	TOTAL	
HN Exclusive deal							
Packages sold	20,000	21,000	22,050	23,152	24,310		1
Average price per package (SK $)	800	800	800	800	800		
Total package revenue (SK $'000)	16,000	16,800	17,640	18,522	19,448		1
Commission rate (%)	4	4	4	5	5		
V's commission (SK $'000)	640	672	706	926	972	3,916	2
Non-Exclusive deal							
HN package revenue (SK $'000)	16,000	16,800	17,640	18,522	19,448		
V's commission from HN (@ 2%)	320	336	353	370	389	1,768	1
TL Packages sold	25,000	25,750	26,522	27,318	28,137		1
Average price per package	450	450	450	450	450		
Total package revenue (SK $'000)	11,250	11,588	11,935	12,293	12,662		1
V's commission from TL (@3 %)	338	348	358	369	380	1,792	1
Total commission under non-exclusive deal (SK $'000)	658	684	711	739	769	3,560	1

9

Impact of commission rates – The calculations (above) initially seem to suggest that V benefits from accepting the exclusive deal. However, this is dependent on it achieving the necessary growth in sales of HN's holidays to trigger the higher rate of commission in years 4 and 5.

However, given that C is effectively a new market for V, and for European tourists more generally, there must be some uncertainty as to the level of bookings V will be able to make there.

If V only receives the 4% commission from HN over the 5 year period, its commission income from the exclusive deal would be lower than if it received the non-exclusive commission rate from HN and TL.

[Tutorial note: Total package revenue from HN over the 5 year period is SK$ 88,410. If the commission rate on this figure was reduced to 4%, commissions would fall to SK $3,536. This is now lower than the commissions non-exclusive deal, even before reducing the total package revenue, which would happen in reality if packages sold were less than forecast.]

[Tutorial note: Although the question told you to ignore the ignore the time value of money in the calculations, it could still be valid to note that the commissions V would receive from the non-exclusive deal are likely to exceed those from the exclusive deal in Years 1-3. Even with the variable commission rates, the exclusive deal only generates higher returns in Years 4 and 5 – where the forecasts are exposed to greater risk and uncertainty than those for the earlier years.]

BPP
LEARNING MEDIA

Other opportunities sacrificed – The calculations (above) have assumed that HN and TL are the only two hotels chains which V can book holidays for in C. However, given the drive to increase international tourism in C, it would seem likely that additional hotel chains will open in the next five years, or existing hotel chains will have packages which could be of interest to V's customers. However, if V is tied into the exclusive deal it will not be able to book any packages at any of these hotels.

This could be a problem for the following reasons:

- V could be missing out on potentially high levels of bookings and commissions it could earn from those hotels.

- V could also lose goodwill with the hotels by not generating any bookings for them

- By limiting itself to dealing with one hotel chain, V is severely restricting the holiday choice it is able to offer its customers; for example, HN's hotels are only likely to be suitable for 'Prestige' travel customers, therefore V risks losing younger Adventure-style customers who might want to visit C. If V cannot offer its customers what they want, this could be particularly damaging in relation to customer satisfaction and retention rates.

5 year deal – Additionally, V should note that the initial exclusive deal will only last for 5 years. It is possible that HN could renew the deal at the end of the 5 years, but there is no guarantee about this. This should be considered a risk with the proposal; because if V cannot recruit customers who had previously booked with other hotels in C, then its revenue from holiday bookings in C is likely to fall significantly after the initial 5 year period.

In addition, if the other hotels in C know that V had initially accepted an exclusive deal with HN, they may subsequently offer C lower commission rates than they offer to the holiday companies which were prepared to deal with all the hotels equally.

<u>Recommendation</u>

V should not accept the exclusive deal, because the potential benefits from receiving the higher commission rate are not high enough to outweigh the risk of being tied to selling holidays for one hotel chain only.

(e)

The concept of corporate social responsibility highlights the importance of V considering the social costs and benefits of its actions, as well as fulfilling its economic duty (to make a profit for its owners).

In this case, when making any decisions about the rainforest holidays, V needs to consider the various stakeholder groups who are interested in the decision: including the local communities in Paragonia, environmental/rainforest campaigners, and customers, as well as V's owners and staff. While there are clearly issues to be addressed about the impact that tourism has on the natural environment, it may be possible for tourism to be introduced in an environmentally sustainable way.

<u>CSR issues facing V</u>

Environmental damage – As the number of visitors to Paragonia increases, the impact on the rainforest is also likely to increase; for example as trees are felled to improve transport into the region, or to make space for new hotel accommodation. This would seem to support the argument that 'tourism destroys the very places it seeks to promote.'

However, an alternative to this argument would be that it is the rainforest which visitors (for example, eco-tourists) are coming to see. Therefore, this provides an incentive for the local people not to destroy too much of the forest.

Sustainability of the forests – One of the major issues in relation to development in a physical environment such as the rainforest is how sustainable that development is. For example, in this case, it seems unlikely that when trees are felled to make space for roads, any new trees are planted to offset the impact of the felling. Therefore, whilst V is clearly not directly responsible for the deforestation, it is debatable how far V could view Paragonia as a 'sustainable destination.'

Again, though V might be able to encourage visitors to 'give something back' to the environment. For example, V could include a (voluntary) charge in the price of rainforest holidays which is a donation towards a charity which works to look after the rainforests and manages the planting of new trees in them.

Supporting local communities – The CSR section on V's website talking about contributing positively to local communities. In this respect, V can argue that tourism is contributing to the local communities in Paragonia by providing them with valuable income. From this perspective, V could argue that it could contribute more to the local communities by selling more holidays; although V will need to ensure, as far as it can, that local people are not being exploited by the holiday packages.

Again, however, there could be a concern that as an increasing number of tourists visit the area this could diminish the extent to which V's holidays can guarantee holidaymakers an 'authentic' experience of life in the rainforests of Paragonia.

Customer requirements – As well as considering the interests of the environment and the local community, however, V should also consider the interests of its customers. In this respect, if V refuses to offer customers the holidays they want, this potentially undermine the **economic sustainability of the company**. In turn, this would damaging to a final stakeholder group – the Directors (who are also the owners of the company).

Question 5

Marking scheme

Requirement (a) (i)

Earnings	2
Dividend payout	3
MAXIMUM FOR REQUIREMENT	**5**

Requirement (a) (ii)

Calculations (earnings growth per year and over the whole period)	3
Drop in earnings, slow recovery	2
Reference to financial objective re earnings and on-line investment (2 marks each)	4
MAXIMUM FOR REQUIREMENT	**7**

Requirement (a) (iii)

Comparison to the 80% target	2
Justification of the movements in the ratio	4
Critical review of the policy	2
MAXIMIMUM FOR REQUIREMENT	**6**

Requirement (b) (i)

Scenario A NPV

Call centre (including residual value)	1
Costs in EUR – correctly converted into SK$	2.5
Launch costs – excluding sunk costs	1
Growing SK$ cash outflows	0.5
Tax calculations	2
Discounting & overall NPV	1
	8

Scenario B NPV

Revised growing EUR cash outflows	1
Computing cash flows	1
Discounting & overall NPV	1
	3
Expected value NPV	2
MAXIMUM FOR REQUIREMENT	**13**

Requirement (b) (ii)

Appropriate base figures	2
Cash due on disposal (including timing delay)	2
Explanation of whether or not to abandon	2
MAXIMIMUM FOR REQUIREMENT	**6**

Requirement (b) (iii)

Cruise investment

Strategic and non financial issues	4
Financing issues	2
Impact of Chief Executive's decision to resign	2
Risk issues – Cabaret changing their fees, quality problems at Cabaret	<u>2</u>
	<u>10</u>

Chartered Airline

Evaluation of returns	1
Discussion of risk	<u>4</u>
	<u>5</u>
MAXIMIMUM FOR REQUIREMENT	<u>10</u>

Structure and presentation (1 for heading, 1 for purpose, 1 for tabulated calculations) <u>3</u>

TOTAL FOR QUESTION <u>50</u>

Solution

Requirement (a) (i)

Year ended 30 June	2007	2008	2009	2010	2011	2012
dividend payout	80.0%	20.0%	80.0%	74.9%	73.0%	73.8%
(dividend per share / earnings per share)						
earnings (SK$m)	23.8	20.7	22.5	23.7	24.3	24.0
(earnings per share x no. shares in issue)						

Requirement (a) (ii)

Extra calculations

<u>(aii)</u>

Year ended 30 June	2007	2008	2009	2010	2011	2012
earnings growth		-13.0%	8.7%	5.3%	2.5%	-1.2%
eps growth		-17.9%	8.7%	5.3%	2.5%	-1.2%

total growth over the period

$$g = \sqrt[n]{\frac{latest \ earnings}{earliest \ earnings}} - 1 \qquad \sqrt[5]{\frac{24}{23.8}} - 1 \quad = \quad \textbf{\underline{0.2\%}}$$

The analysis of earnings shows a major fall in earnings between 2007 and 2008 of 13%. This coincides with the heavy investment in V's on-line booking service which may have caused extra costs in form of higher interest payment on money borrowed to finance the investment (although some of the finance was raised by more shares being issued, which is why the fall in eps is higher at -17.9%). Some of the fall in earnings may also be accounted for by the on-going loss of market share and potentially by economic factors as well.

Earnings recovered strongly in 2008, showing a growth in total earnings of 8.7%. Annual growth in earnings subsequently fell back to 5.3% in 2010 and to just 2.5% in 2011 before falling slightly in 2012. This may reflect the benefits of the new online systems but if so these benefits are being eroded over time.

V's earnings growth target of 5% was only met in 2009 and 2010. Taking the period as a whole earnings only grew on average by 0.2% p.a. and so the performance of V over this period can be viewed as disappointing but reference to its financial objective to grow earnings by 5% per year which is the only yardstick that is available.

Requirement (a) (iii)

In 2007 V was paying out 80% of profits as dividend, as per V's objective. Following this the payout fell dramatically to 20%, which occurred in the year in which the investment in on-line systems was made. The rationale for this is likely to be that cutting the dividend is logical for a company in a year in which an important strategic investment is due to be made which will bring long-term benefits to shareholders.

Again in 2009 V returned to its 80% payout policy, a policy that looks high but could be justified for a limited company whose shareholders will not be able to sell shares on the open market and who will want some return for the risks that they are taking. There is, however, a risk attached to such a policy as it significantly reduces the value of funds available for re-investment which could damage long term growth prospects. It also increases the possible need for additional debt finance, which is not necessarily very easy to obtain in a period where credit is in short supply due to the economic downturn and increasing capital requirements for banks.

After 2009 the dividend payout has fallen, which perhaps indicates that 80% dividend payout is not affordable at this point in time. In fact the dividend per share has been constant (even when V's earnings have fallen in 2012). The rationale for such a policy is likely to be to provide stability to shareholders. Such a policy (of dropping the payout ratio) would also be helpful if a company is trying to conserve capital for use in the proposed expansion plans.

Requirement (b) (i)

Appendix to report

Appendix - analysis of the cruise project
Scenario A

	01-Jan-13					
Time	0	1	2	3	4	Notes
SK$ million						
Revenue		7.4	7.6	7.8	8.0	growing at 3% per year
Payment to Cabaret		-1.2	-1.3	-1.4	-1.5	see working
SK$ operating costs		-2.0	-2.1	-2.2	-2.3	ignoring research as a sunk cost
net		4.1	4.2	4.2	4.2	growing at 5% per year
tax paid		-1.2	-1.2	-1.3	-1.3	at 30%
call centre	-6.8					
tax saved		2.0				time 0 is the start of this tax year
launch	-3.0					
tax saved		0.9				
residual value					4.0	
tax paid					-1.2	
net	-9.8	5.8	2.9	2.9	5.8	
df 15%	1.000	0.870	0.756	0.658	0.572	
pv	-9.8	5.1	2.2	1.9	3.3	
NPV	2.7					

Workings

Time	0	1	2	3	4	
EUR million						
costs		-1.0	-1.1	-1.1	-1.2	growing at 5% per year
ex rate	1.200	1.224	1.248	1.273	1.299	x 1.02 per year
SK$m		-1.2	-1.3	-1.4	-1.5	

Scenario B

Time	01-Jan-13 0	1	2	3	4	Notes
SK$ million						
Revenue		3.7	3.8	3.9	4.0	growing at 3% per year
Payment to Cabaret		-1.2	-1.3	-1.4	-1.5	as scenario A
SK$ operating costs		-1.5	-1.6	-1.7	-1.7	growing at 5% per year
net		1.0	0.9	0.9	0.8	
tax paid		-0.3	-0.3	-0.3	-0.2	at 30%
call centre	-6.8					as scenario A
tax saved		2.0				as scenario A
launch	-3.0					as scenario A
tax saved		0.9				as scenario A
residual value					4.0	as scenario A
tax paid					-1.2	as scenario A
net	**-9.8**	**3.6**	**0.6**	**0.6**	**3.4**	
df 15%	1.000	0.870	0.756	0.658	0.572	
pv	-9.8	3.1	0.5	0.4	1.9	
NPV	**-3.8**					

average NPV	0.7	(0.7 x NPV scenario A + 0.3 x NPV scenario B)

this is an expected value

Requirement (b) (ii)

Appendix to report

scenario b

Time	01-Jan-13 0	1	2	Notes
net cash inflows		1.0		as scenario B
tax paid		-0.3		as scenario B
call centre	-6.8	5.7		
tax saved		2.0	-1.7	
launch	-3.0			as scenario B
tax saved		0.9		as scenario B
net	-9.8	9.3	-1.7	
df 15%	1.000	0.870	0.756	
pv	-9.8	8.1	-1.3	
NPV	**-3.0**			

Other approaches are possible here.

Alternative solution
Do not abandon

	01-Jan-14				
Time	0	1	2	3	Notes
SK$ million					
net		0.9	0.8	0.8	as scenario B
tax paid		-0.3	-0.2	-0.2	
residual value				4.0	
tax paid				-1.2	
net	**0.0**	**0.6**	**0.6**	**3.4**	
df 15%	1.000	0.870	0.756	0.658	
pv	0.0	0.5	0.4	2.2	
NPV	**3.2**				

Abandon

	01-Jan-14	
Time	0	1
SK$ million		
residual value	5.7	
tax paid		-1.7
net	**5.7**	**-1.7**
df 15%	1.000	0.870
pv	5.7	-1.5
NPV	**4.2**	

Answers

REPORT

To: The Board of V

From: Management Accountant

Date: xxxx

Re: Proposed Investment Strategy

Introduction and purpose

Two proposals have been put forward: to launch cruise holidays, or to acquire a chartered airline. This report considers the details of these proposals, which are understood to be mutually exclusive because V does not have the resources to undertake both at the same time, and concludes with a recommendation.

SECTION (i) FINANCIAL ANALYSIS OF THE CRUISE INVESTMENT

Scenario A (optimistic scenario 70% chance)	Net Present Value + SK$ 2.7 million
Scenario B (pessimistic scenario 30% chance)	Net Present Value – SK$ 3.8 million
Expected value	Net Present Value + SK$ 0.75 million

This analysis is attached as an appendix to this report.

A positive net present value (NPV) indicates that the project is delivering a return that is higher than the 15% cost of capital. The expected value includes the probability of scenario A (70%) and scenario B (30%).

Conclusion:

The investment in cruises provides attractive returns under scenario A and also using a weighted average that takes into account the likelihood of scenarios A and B. However, the project does not provide attractive returns under scenario B, although this ignores the potential benefit of the option to abandon which is discussed below.

SECTION (ii) WHETHER TO ABANDON THE CRUISE INVESTMENT UNDER SCENARIO B

We know that it would be possible to abandon the project at the end of the first year without penalty and retain the ability to realise a residual value of SK$ 5.7 million on the investment in the call centre. This would however be subject to a balancing charge in respect of tax depreciation allowances already claimed.

As shown in the appendix, the present value of project under scenario B improves by approximately SK$ 1 million (from SK$-3.8 million to SK$ - 3 million) if the project is abandoned.

However in reality the attractiveness of this option is limited because of the impact on V's reputation and the damage that this move could cause to staff morale which is a strength of V's.

Conclusion:

There are strong arguments for continuing with the project rather than abandoning it on 1 January 2014, even if Scenario B holds true for the remaining term of the project.

SECTION (iii) ADVISE ON WHETHER TO PROCEED WITH EITHER INVESTMENT

Cruise investment

The cruise investment would appear to build on the expertise and success of our Prestige Travel operation. This is a growing sector of the holiday market and has been successfully penetrated by many small independent travel agents, for example Bath Travel. The main strategic risk would be the relationship with Cabaret which would need to be carefully vetted to ensure that a trading relationship with Cabaret would not create unacceptable reputational risk for V.

Although the returns from the investment are only marginally attractive in expected value terms (+ SK$ 0.75 million) it should be noted that expected values are indicative of the 'long-run average' return that would be expected if this investment decision was taken repeatedly. In fact this is a one-off decision and, as such, it is the positive NPV of +SK$2.7 million under scenario A that is of more interest. In scenario A the payback is also less than 3 years which indicates that this is likely to be a fairly low risk project. Finally, in the unexpected event of the project not succeeding there is the possibility of using the option to abandon which would allow us to recoup the bulk of the cash flows from our investment; albeit at some cost to our reputation and staff relationships.

Chartered airline

The acquisition of a small airline would be an unusual strategic move. Where this has been attempted by similar companies to V, such as Bath Travel, it has not been successful because the airline has faced massive competitive pressures from low-cost operators such as easyJet who are aggressively expanding in most European markets. It is not in line with V's stated intention to broaden its product range.

The returns are potentially higher than the cruises investment (SK$ 5 million vs SK$ 2.7 million) but the risk is higher too.

Finally it should be noted that the outlay required for this investment is about 50% (SK$ 5.2 million) higher than the cruises investment. This may be important if V needs to conserve cash to pay dividends (dividends have not grown in the past few years) or to repay 30% of its bank borrowings in 2 years time. The Chief Executive may also be reluctant to commit heavily to a risky investment within 1 year of retirement.

Conclusion

In summary, it is recommended that V does not pursue the airline acquisition opportunity but instead channels its investment into diversifying its product range by making a strong strategic move into the cruise holidays market.

Question 6

Marking scheme

	Marks
Requirement (a) (i)	
Calculation of appropriate cost of equity	3
DVM calculation using V financial objectives for growth and dividend payout	4
DVM calculation using A plc financial objectives for growth and dividend payout	3
MAXIMUM FOR REQUIREMENT	**8**
Requirement (a) (ii)	
P/E valuation using proxy (no growth, growth, appropriate adjustment for unlisted)	2
P/E valuation using A plc (no growth, growth, appropriate adjustment for unlisted)	1
MAXIMUM FOR REQUIREMENT	**3**
Requirement (a) (iii)	
Relevance of DVM valuation	1
Limitations of DVM (appropriate Ke, use of proxy, appropriate growth rate)	Max 3
Relevance of P/E valuation	1
Limitations of P/E method (appropriate P/E, adjusted P/E, appropriate earnings figure)	Max 3
MAXIMUM FOR REQUIREMENT	**7**
Requirement (b)	
Determination of terms of bid	1
Calculation of total number of shares post-merger	1
Calculation of A plc cost of equity using DVM	3
Calculation of integration costs using DCF	4
Valuation of A plc	1
Combined post-merger value (total company and per share)	2
MAXIMUM FOR REQUIREMENT	**12**
Requirement (c)	
Appropriate valuation for trade sale to A plc (DVM, P/E, DCF)	4
Share value for IPO (DVM, P/E, DCF)	4
Conclusion	2
MAXIMUM FOR REQUIREMENT	**7**

Requirement (d)

Advantages of stock market listing	2
Disadvantages of stock market listing	2
Advantages of trade sale	2
Disadvantages of trade sale	2
Alternative financing options	2
Recommendations	2

MAXIMUM FOR REQUIREMENT **<u>10</u>**

Structure and presentation (1 for heading, 1 for purpose, 1 for tabulated calculations) <u>3</u>

TOTAL FOR QUESTION <u>50</u>

REPORT

To: The Board of V

From: External Consultant

Date: November 2012

Re: Trade Sales versus IPO

Introduction and purpose

A proposal has been put forward to raise finance for the future development of the business by either a trade sale or a flotation on the stock market. This report considers the details of these proposals based on various scenarios and evaluates what action, if any, should be taken.

The report also considers the wider implications of the proposal – that is, the effects on the company – and concludes with a recommendation.

SECTION A: Valuation of V

(i) Dividend Valuation Model (DVM)

V is a private, unlisted entity and therefore does not have a current share price and the cost of equity is difficult to determine. By using the Dividend Valuation Method, the cost of equity can be determined by identifying a comparable quoted company and adjusting the known equity beta for the different gearing structures between the two companies.

From the calculations shown in Appendix (i) we can estimate V's cost of equity to be 12%.

On the assumption that V's earnings growth objective of 5 % is a reasonable estimate of dividend growth and that 80% of profits are paid as dividends the current dividend is estimated at SK\$24m x 80% = SK\$19.2m, then:

$$P_0 = \frac{d_0(1+g)}{K_e-g} = \frac{19.2m(1+0.05)}{0.12-0.05} = \text{SK\$288m in total or SK\$3.20 per share}$$

A plc have stated that under their management, V could grow earnings by 10% per annum, and if acquired by V it is assumed that the 70% payout ratio of A plc. would be adopted. Therefore, valuations on this basis would be:

$$P_0 = \frac{d_0(1+g)}{K_e-g} = \frac{24m \times 70\% \times (1+0.1)}{0.12-0.10} = \text{SK\$924m in total or SK\$10.27 per share}$$

(ii) Earnings valuation

Valuation = P/E Ratio x Earnings

Using a comparable quoted company (Proxy):

Valuation = 13 x SK\$24m = SK\$312m total company or SK\$3.47 per share

Reduce by multiplying the P/E by 2/3 as V is an unlisted company: SK\$208m total company or SK\$2.31 per share

If synergies realised: 13 x SK\$24m x 1.1 = SK\$ 343.2m total company or SK\$3.81 per share

Reduce by 2/3 as V is an unlisted company: SK$ 228.8m total company or SK$2.54 per share

Further valuations are provided in Appendix (ii).

Finally, if synergies realised following acquisition allowing A plc.'s P/E ratio to be used then:

Valuation =37 x SK$24m x 1.1 = SK$976.8m total company or SK$10.85 per share

(iii) Relevance and limitations of DVM versus P/E Valuation

The Dividend Valuation Method values a company based on the forecast future dividends of the company. It is regularly used for listed companies to assess if the shares are under or overvalued but is commonly used to value minority share-holdings.

V is not listed and therefore there are a number of limitations for use of this model for this scenario. It is not easy to determine the cost of equity to be used in the DVM. It is therefore necessary to identify a proxy company and calculated an assumed cost of equity based by adjustment of the proxy company's equity beta. This should be reasonably accurate if the proxy company is in the same industry, of a similar size and at the same stage in its business lifecycle.

In the calculations above, Proxy plc's equity beta has been used. Proxy plc also operates in the travel industry, and with 70 outlets throughout SK, is of a similar size and operational risk. It is unclear what stage of the business lifecycle Proxy plc is in and this may require further assessment.

The P/E basis of company valuation determines the value of a company based on the market's expectations of future growth in earnings of that company.

However, since V is not listed, it does not currently have a known share price and therefore does not have an easily calculated P/E ratio. There also needs to be some consideration of the relevant earnings figure to use. The latest earnings are known, and would usually be considered a reasonable guide to future earnings.

In summary the DVM would appear to give the best indicator of V's value because of the problems in finding a suitable P/E ratio.

SECTION B: EVALUATE THE EXPECTED POST-MERGER VALUE AND SHARE PRICE OF P PLC. AND CALCULATE THE OUTCOME OF THE PROPOSED SHARE FOR SHARE EXCHANGE.

Terms of Bid

A plc has a current share price of SK$43.50 and has offered SK$4.50 per share to the existing V shareholders.

Share for Share exchange = SK$43.50/SK$4.50 = 9.67 V shares per A plc share, so approximately 10 shares

So the total number of shares post-merger will be:

$\frac{90m \text{ V shares}}{10 \text{ V/A plc.}}$ = 9m new A plc shares, plus 100m existing A plc shares = 109m shares post-merger

The value of acquisition to A plc

From section A (i) of this report, the value of V under A plc's ownership can be estimated at SK$ 924 million (using the DVM). However this acquisition will incur integration costs, which need to be evaluated:

This requires calculation of the expected post-merger cash flows, including synergies, discounted at A plc's cost of equity

Using DVM, $K_e = \frac{d_0(1 + g)}{P_0} + g$ $= \frac{SK\$119m/100m \ x \ 70\% \ x \ 1.07}{SK\$43.50} + 7\% = $ approx. 9%

Where latest dividend = SK$119m earnings/100m shares x 70% dividend payout ratio

Target growth rate for A plc is 7% therefore g = 7%

Discounted Cash flow (SK$m)

Year ended 30th June	2013	2014	2015
Integration costs	(10.00)	(7.00)	(1.00)
Tax saved	3.00	2.10	0.30
NCF	(7.00)	(4.90)	(0.70)
Annuity (1/r)			11.111
Value at time 2 (2014)			(7.78)
DF@9%	0.917	0.842	0.842
PV	(6.42)	(4.13)	(6.55)

Total NPV =   SK$ (17.1m)

NPV = post-merger value V   SK$924m

Current market value of A plc   SK$ = 43.50 x 100m shares = SK$4350m

Therefore total post-merger value of A plc = (17) + 924 + 4350 = SK$5257m or (5257 / 109) = SK$48.23 per share

SECTION C: ADVICE ON APPROPRIATE VALUATION IN NEGOTIATIONS WITH A PLC.

The valuation methods used in section A of this report give a wide range of values. This section advises on which values would be appropriate to use in negotiations over a sale price with A plc.

DVM

A major consideration for the use of the DVM is the growth rate and dividend value to use. The calculations in part (a) provide a range of DVM values of SK$288m to SK$924m. If V pursues the stock market flotation, then it seems reasonable to use the predicted growth and dividend payout ratio that the Executive Chairman indicated in his press statement. However, these are not currently being achieved and this forecast is based on an estimate only. A valuation on this basis must therefore be used with some caution. This would give a value of SK$288m, although it is usual to offer for sale at a discount when conducting an Initial Public Offering to encourage purchase of the shares and to reflect the reality the current unlisted status of the shares.

If the trade sale is to be pursued, then it seems reasonable to use the growth rate predicted by A plc. and their dividend payout ratio. Since A plc is a large, vertically integrated operator, there is an assumption that A plc has previously completed successful integrations of similar companies to V and that their forecast of 10% growth would be based on this. However, A plc is only achieving 7% growth overall and therefore it may be too optimistic that the growth in earnings related to V would continue to grow at 10% indefinitely beyond the initial integration and investment phase.

P/E Basis

This is a useful valuation method, especially when considering the IPO, as it indicates what the market would pay for a share in the company. When considering the proposed trade sale to A plc, which is also in the same industry, it may seem more appropriate to use the P/E ratio of A plc, as it is this proven management team who will control and manage V following integration. It therefore also gives a good indication of the value A plc should be prepared to pay for the shares in V. The calculations in part (a) provide a range of earnings values of SK$208m to SK$977m. The P/E basis suggests that A plc should be likely to consider a bid of up to SK$977m reasonable given their predictions for increased growth potential for V within the integrated structure of A plc. However, this seems unlikely given the marked difference between this figure and those calculated by the DVM and DCF valuations.

When considering a stock market flotation, it is common practice to use the industry average P/E ratio and apply an adjustment. The information is not available for the industry average P/E ratio, but it seems reasonable to use the P/E ratio of Proxy plc as it is a company in the same industry and of a similar size and business risk. However, since Proxy plc is listed and V is not, it would be possible to apply an adjustment to reduce the P/E ratio to reflect the current lack of marketability of V, but any adjustment applied is purely arbitrary. It could also be argued that V may have a higher growth potential than Proxy plc, at least initially, and therefore the adjustment could be to increase the P/E ratio used.

The relevance of the earnings figure used must also be considered. Given the current proposal is for a stock market flotation or a trade sale, with the main focus on achieving funding for future development and growth, there is a good argument for the use of a forecast earnings figure to be used in place of the most recent earnings. For the trade sale proposal, it would seem more relevant to use A plc's forecast of 10% growth to apply to the current earnings, whereas for the stock market flotation the more modest figure of 5% as estimated by the Executive Chairman gives an indication of what V believe is realistically achievable.

Discounted cash flows

DCF can give a useful measure of the value of a company, particularly in respect of an acquisition or merger where synergies can be realised. The forecast future earnings can be used as an approximation of the free cash flows for V. These need to be discounted at an appropriate cost of capital. It is common practice to use the cost of equity, but this is difficult to calculate for an unlisted company such as V.

In addition, the DCF valuation has been based on cash flows generated in perpetuity, which can provide an unrealistically high valuation. It may be useful in terms of estimating the maximum value that A plc. could achieve following integration of V and therefore a maximum indicate value. A plc. certainly would not pay more than this to obtain V.

In the calculation in part (b) the cost of equity for A plc as a whole was calculated and used for the discounting. This is highly subjective, but since it is the existing shareholders of A plc who will be taking on the risk of achieving these cash flows it seems reasonable to use this to establish an acceptable maximum price that A plc would be prepared to pay to acquire V.

SECTION D: RECOMMENDATION

A trade sale

This would effectively be a takeover of V by a competitor, A plc. The directors of V would receive shares in A plc, which could be an attractive proposition as they will also retain their employment. As so much of the value of the company comes from the expertise of its directors and employees, the directors could expect to be tied into a contract with the competitor for a period of time. The disadvantage for these directors is that they would lose control of their business and have to follow the strategy and policies of the competitor. The Operations Director seems keen to take this option rather than the IPO which suggests he may be looking for the potential career development that a larger organisation may provide.

An initial public offering (IPO)

The main attraction of an IPO is that the original owners of a company are able to realise the value of their holding. It also enables future growth of the company by allowing access to a wider pool of finance, and can be seen to enhance the public image of the company, improving the marketability of the shares and making it easier to seek growth by acquisition. However, IPOs are expensive due to brokerage commissions and underwriting fees. Their success is dependent on trading conditions in the market at the time of flotation, which are currently poor due to the volatility of the stock market over the last few years. There will also be significantly greater public regulation, director accountability and scrutiny and a wider circle of investors with more exacting requirements will hold shares. V would also need to be able to convince investors that future growth is achievable given that recent performance has not shown much growth.

Recommendation

Given the uncertainty in the current economic outlook it is recommended that V should sell out to a competitor and maximise the value of their holding now.

APPENDIX

(i) Estimate of V's cost of equity

Step 1: Use proxy company beta 1.4 and ungear

$\beta_u = \beta_g[V_e /(V_e + V_d (1-t))] = 1.4[85/(85 + 15(1-0.3))] = 1.246$

Step 2: Regear the beta to determine beta for V

$\beta_g = \beta_u + (\beta_u + \beta_d)(V_d(1-t)/V_e) = 1.246 + (1.246 + 0)(50(1-0.3)/75) = 1.827$

Step 3: Use geared beta to calculate K_e using CAPM

$K_e = R_f + (R_m - R_f)\beta_g = 3\% + (8\% - 3\%)1.827 = 12.135\%$, say 12%

(ii) Earnings valuation

If this sell-off allows V to realise their financial objective of 5% earnings growth per year on average:

Valuation = 13 x SK\$24m x 105% = SK\$327.6m total company or SK\$3.64 per share

Reduce by 2/3 as V is an unlisted company: SK\$218.4m total company or SK\$2.43 per share

Using A plc P/E ratio:

Valuation = 37 x SK\$24m = SK\$888m total company or SK\$9.87 per share

Question 7

Marking scheme

	Marks
Requirement (a) (i)	
Revenue	2
Operating costs	1.5
Redundancy cost	0.5
Profit on disposal	1
Legal costs	2
Interest income	0.5
Finance costs	0.5
Income tax	1
Non-current assets	1.5
Inventories	0.5
Trade and other receivables	1
Cash and cash equivalents (Balancing figure)	1
Share capital and share premium	0.5
Retained earnings	1.5
Long-term borrowings	1
Revenue received in advance (non-current)	0.5
Trade and other payables	1
Revenue received in advance (current)	1
Comment on limitations of forecast	2
MAXIMUM FOR REQUIREMENT	**18**
Requirement (a) (ii)	
Calculation of dividend payout ratio	1
Comment on dividend payout	2
Calculation of earnings growth	1
Comment on earnings growth	2
Comment on general financial performance (up to two marks per valid point)	4
MAXIMUM FOR REQUIREMENT	**10**
Requirement (a) (iii)	
Comment on gearing ratio throughout period	2
Comment on shortage of cash at 30 June 2014	2
MAXIMUM FOR REQUIREMENT	**4**
Requirement (a) (iv)	
Discussion of equity (listing and rights issue)	3
Venture capital	1
Debt finance	2
Sale and leaseback	1
Leasing	1
MAXIMUM FOR REQUIREMENT	**7**
Requirement (b)	
Dividend objective	2 - 3
Earnings growth objective	1 - 2
Asset turnover	1 - 2
Range of measures proposal	1 - 2
MAXIMUM FOR REQUIREMENT	**8**
Structure and presentation	**3**
TOTAL FOR QUESTION	**50**

Suggested solution

REPORT

To: Board of Directors, V

From: Financial Adviser

Date: 1 December 2012

Re: Expansion of V and forecast results

Introduction

This report focuses on the proposed expansion of V and the forecast effect on financial results.

The first part of the report calculates the forecast financial results for the years ending 30 June 2013 and 30 June 2014.

The second part of the report then looks at the financial performance of V in the forecast period and also considers whether the financial objectives of V have been met or not. The report also considers the capital structure of V during the forecast period and assesses any need for additional finance for V.

The final part of this report considers alternative sources of finance for V to fund the proposed expansion.

(a) (i) Forecast Income statement and statement of financial position

The full forecast financial statements can be found in appendix 1. Note that where annual growth percentages were given, that this growth has been apportioned for the six months from 1 January to 30 June 2013 and a full year of growth for the year ended 30 June 2014.

The major limitation with the forecast is that it has been based estimates of growth and trends which may turn out to be inaccurate. Given that we are already part way through the year ended 30 June 2013 these figures are likely to be more accurate than those for the year ended 30 June 2014. The risk of inaccuracy could be mitigated by carrying out detailed sensitivity analysis on the key variables and seeing the impact on V. In addition there are external factors which could impact the assumptions on which the forecast has been based, for example if a major competitor to V goes out of business, then V's financial performance could improve.

(a) (ii) Financial performance of V

General performance

Overall V remains profitable in the forecast period, although net operating profit is reduced as a result of the falling margin due to V not passing on all cost increases to the customer.

The one-off items in 2013 means that profit is slightly distorted in that year and there is an overall increase of SK$2 million, meaning that profit after tax is almost the same as in the previous year. Profit after tax then falls by SK$2.5 million from 2013 to 2014.

Cash as at 30 June 2014 does not appear to be high enough to support ongoing operations in view of the volatile nature of cash flows in the travel industry.

Financial objectives

The calculations of the relevant ratios for the financial objectives can be found in appendix 2. It can be seen that the dividend payout ratio is higher than the stated objective of 80% of earnings in all three years. However it should be noted that in 2014 the dividend payout is forecast to be greater than earnings, meaning that part of the payout is paid out of retained earnings, which cannot be sustained in the long run. The level of dividend payouts may need to be reviewed and there is scope to reduce the payments and for them still to be in line with the stated objective.

Earnings, measured by profit after tax, are falling year on year, with a substantial fall of more than 10% in the year ended 30 June 2014. This means that the stated objective of 5% growth has not been achieved in either year or in total across the period. The period under review may be too short to draw any conclusion about long-term growth prospects, but the directors may need to investigate further expansion opportunities in order to achieve this objective in the long term.

(a) (iii) Capital structure and financing needs

The capital structure of V is restricted by the covenant on the existing debt which states that long-term debt divided by long-term debt plus equity cannot be more than 50%. This means that the amount of long-term debt cannot exceed the amount of equity. Under the forecast, V is not scheduled to break this covenant at any stage.

At 30 June 2014 the gearing ratio is [35 / (78 +35)] = 31% which means there is scope for V to increase its borrowing. It may wish to renew the borrowing facility of the SK$15 million which is due to be repaid on 30 June 2014 as the repayment means that there will only be SK$1.7 million of cash left for V, which is unlikely to be enough to sustain day-to-day operations given the volatile nature of the cash balance of V.

If V decides not to renew the borrowing facility, or is unable to do so then it will need to seek additional financing to be able to meet operational needs.

(a) (iv) Sources of finance

There are a number of alternative sources of finance for V to finance the proposed expansion, which would allow all of the branches to be retained, but not all of them would be appropriate in the circumstances.

A stock market listing would be a way of raising finance, but it would have to be considered whether the current economic conditions would make a successful listing difficult. In any case, a stock market listing is a lengthy process and the funds would not be realised in time to finance the proposed expansion on 1 January 2013.

An issue of equity to existing shareholders in the form of a rights issue may be possible in the time, but this would depend on whether the shareholders are willing to invest more in the company, particularly in the case of the Chief Executive who has stated his intention to sell his shareholding at the end of the year ended 30 June 2013.

Venture capitalists are not likely to want to get involved in V as it is not a young, high-growth company and there is not the opportunities for them to get the level of return they would require.

Debt finance is only likely to be available through a bank loan, or similar, as V is not in a position to issue its own debt. Debt finance is available to V, under the debt covenant in place V could borrow up to SK$25 million more at 30 June 2012. However, any provider of debt finance would have to be convinced about the creditworthiness of V before agreeing to the borrowing. This seems likely and in addition V appears to have sufficient non-current assets that could be offered as security.

Given the amount of Vs non-current assets (SK$123 million at 30 June 2012) it seems feasible that sale and leaseback of some of the assets could be used to raise the SK$15 million needed for the expansion.

Finally, the dividends paid in 2013 and 2014 could be reduced from the expected levels and still meet the financial objective of paying out 80%. The minimum level to meet this objective would mean dividends of SK$19 million in 2013 and SK$17 million in 2014. This would save SK$6 million in cash (SK$1.5 million in 2013 and SK$4 million in 2014), but is probably not enough to prevent the need for other financing.

Although there are not enough details to assess this, there may be a possibility that V can lease some of the assets required for the expansion and therefore they would not have to pay for them upfront, so less financing would be required.

Conclusion

This report has calculated the forecast performance of V over a two year period, and evaluated the financial performance. Further investment and expansion is likely to be needed to achieve the long-term earnings growth objective that has been set by the board. In addition, further financing or a renewal of the debt to be repaid on 30 June 2014 will be necessary in order to maintain day-to-day operations.

There are other possible sources of financing the proposed expansion, of which the most appropriate are either further debt borrowing or sale and leaseback of non-current assets.

If you have any questions relating to any part of this report please do not hesitate to contact me.

Appendices

Appendix 1 – Forecast financial statements

Income statement

	2012	2013	2014	
Revenue	250.0	253.8	261.4	Growth of 3% per year
				Initial ratio = 215/250 = 86%. Ratio increases by 1% each
Operating Costs	-215.0	-220.8	-230.0	year
Net operating profit	35.0	33.0	31.4	
Redundancy payment		-2.0		
Profit on asset disposal		9.0		Difference between net book value and price paid
Legal cost		-5.0		
Interest income	3.0	3.0	3.0	No change
Finance costs	-4.0	-4.0	-4.0	No change
Corporate income tax	-10.0	-10.2	-9.1	30% of profit before tax
Profit for the year	24.0	23.8	21.3	

Statement of financial position

	2012	2013	2014	
Non-current assets	123.0	127.5	122.0	2013 NBV bf - nbv of assets sold + assets purchased - dep
Current assets				
Inventories	3.0	3.7	3.7	
Trade and other receivables	70.0	74.2	77.2	Increase of 6% then 4%
Cash and cash equivalents	37.0	17.8	1.7	
Total current assets	110.0	95.7	82.5	
Total assets	233.0	223.2	204.5	
Equity and liabilities				
Equity				
Share capital	9.0	9.0	9.0	No change
Share premium	6.0	6.0	6.0	No change
Retained earnings	60.0	63.3	63.0	Add profit for the year less dividends
Total equity	75.0	78.3	78.0	

Non-current liabilities

Long-term borrowings	50.0	35.0	35.0	Repayment of SK$15m on 30 June 2014, becomes current in 2013
Revenue received in advance	3.0	2.2	2.2	
Current liabilities				
Trade and other payables	35.0	28.0	25.2	Falls by 20% then 10%
Borrowing to be repaid 2014		15.0		
Revenue received in advance	70.0	64.8	64.1	Falls by 7.5% then 1%
Total liabilities	158.0	145.0	126.5	
Total equity and liabilities	233.0	223.2	204.5	

Appendix 2 – Financial objectives

Ratio of earnings paid out as dividends

	2012	2013	2014
PAT	24	23.8	21.3
Div	19.5	20.5	21.5
Ratio	81.3%	86.1%	100.9%

Increase in earnings

	2012	2013	2014
PAT	24	23.8	21.3
Earnings growth		-0.9%	-10.7%

(b) There are only two current financial objectives for V: the dividend payout should be 80% of earnings and earnings (on average) should be growing at 5% per year.

The objective of paying out 80% of earnings as dividends may be appropriate for an unlisted company that does not require reinvestment of funds, but with the current expansion plans this does not appear to be a sensible policy. The payment of large dividends may mean that the company then needs to borrow to fund the expansion when it had actually generated sufficient funds to finance the expansion anyway. Perhaps a lower payout ratio of 30% would be more appropriate in V's current position.

The current incentive scheme rewarding achieving 5% growth in earnings each year could reward short-termism and encourage managers to make short-term decisions to achieve 5% growth in the current year rather than make a decision that would increase earnings in future years. It should be noted that the objective is the seek average growth of 5%, but that the incentive scheme will make managers focus on the current year.

Asset turnover is probably most applicable in a capital intensive production business. Although V has a large amount of non-current assets it could be argued that these do not necessarily drive the financial performance of the business and therefore to use them as part of an important performance measure would be misleading.

It is not appropriate for any performance measure for V to be based on share price as V is an unlisted company. No one performance measure on its own can be a definitive measure of company financial performance, but V could use a range of measures such as return on capital employed, profit margin and cash operating cycle which could be compared to a competitor or to an industry benchmark to assess relative performance. In practice it may be difficult to determine a suitable competitor or benchmark and to find the necessary comparable information. Benchmarking databases are available such as for the centre for inter-firm comparisons. It is also true that larger quoted companies would be easier to benchmark against but these are likely to be less relevant for comparison to a small company.

BPP
LEARNING MEDIA

Question 8

Marking scheme

	Marks
Requirement (a)	
Compound annualised post tax cost of debt calculation	2
NPV of lease payments	2
Tax saving on capital allowances	2
NPV of purchasing aircraft	2
Analysis of lease versus buy	<u>1</u>
Breakeven cost of borrowing calculation	<u>2</u>
MAXIMUM FOR REQUIREMENT	<u>11</u>
Requirement (b) (i)	
Conclusion on part (a) results	1
Sensitivity to interest rate	3
Calculation	3
Discussion Sensitivity to residual value	3
Sensitivity calculation	
Discussion	3
Other factors	3
	4
Recommendation	2
MAXIMUM FOR REQUIREMENT	<u>15</u>
Requirement (b) (ii)	
One mark per valid point	
MAXIMUM FOR REQUIREMENT	<u>6</u>
Requirement (c)	
Up to 2 marks per fully explained point	
MAXIMUM FOR REQUIREMENT	<u>8</u>
Requirement (d)	
Up to 2 marks per fully explained point	
MAXIMUM FOR REQUIREMENT	<u>7</u>
Presentation marks (1 for headings, 1 for purpose, 1 for presentation of calculations)	<u>3</u>
TOTAL FOR QUESTION	<u>50</u>

Suggested solution

REPORT

To: Board of Directors, V

From: Financial Adviser

Date: 1 December 2012

Re: Acquisition of aircraft

Introduction

The purpose of this report is to evaluate whether it would be better for V to purchase or lease the two aircraft. The report individually appraises the purchase and lease options from a financial perspective including some sensitivity analysis. The report goes on to consider whether a wet lease is a better option than the initial two options proposed.

Finally the report will consider the advantages and disadvantages of post-completion audits and advise on their suitability for V.

Section A

(a)   (i)   Compound annualised post-tax cost of debt

The 6 month reference rate is 4.2% for a 6 month period. This is a compound annualised pre-tax cost of $1.042^2 - 1 = 8.57\%$. The company's rate is 1% pa above this, which is 9.57% per annum.

The after tax cost will therefore be 9.57% $(1 - 0.3) = 6.70\%$.

(ii)   NPV of lease versus purchase decision at 6% and 7%

The PV of the lease payments after tax relief, at 6% and 7%,have been calculated in appendix 1. The lease is assumed to be an operating lease because the lessor retains the risk of loss on the residual value of the aircraft.

The PV of purchasing the aircraft has also been estimated at 6% and 7% and the full calculation can be found in appendix 2.

These calculations show that the additional present value of cost expected if the planes are purchased rather than leased is expected to be:

At 6% cost of borrowing (SK$000s): 3,489.8 − 3,361.5 = 128.3.
At 7% cost of borrowing (SK$000s): 3,631.6 − 3,314.9 = 316.7.

(iii)   The breakeven post tax cost of debt at which there is no difference between the cost of leasing and the cost of purchasing will be lower than 6% and can be estimated by extrapolating these results.

Break-even cost of borrowing = 6% + [128.3 / (128.3 − 316.7)] × 1% = 5.3%.

Section B

(b)   (i)   Purchase or lease

On the basis of the above figures, if the company's post tax borrowing rate is 6.7%, **leasing is** cheaper than purchasing, but this needs to be investigated further by looking at the sensitivity of the decision to some key variables.

Sensitivity to the reference 6-month SK$ inter-bank rate

Leasing is cheaper unless V's post tax cost of debt falls to 5.3% pa. This is a pre-tax rate of 5.3% / 0.7 = 7.57% pa.

Subtracting 1% per annum premium implies an annual inter-bank rate of 6.57%

This implies a 6-month rate of $1.0657^{0.5} - 1 = 3.23\%$ per 6 month period.

This means that for the loan to be more attractive than the lease the maximum reference 6-month SK$ inter-bank rate is 3.23%, compared with the present figure of 4.2%.

Thus if interest rates fall more than 97 basis points (0.97% decrease), leasing will be more expensive.

Sensitivity to the residual value

The project is extremely sensitive to the residual value of the aircraft, which has be noted to be uncertain, with the possibility that it could be significantly lower, depending on the state of the airline industry. The sensitivity of the residual value of the aircraft is calculated as 10.3% (see appendix 3 for full calculation).

Thus, not only is leasing expected to be cheaper, it does not carry interest rate risk and the risk of a fall in the planes' residual value.

Other factors

Other factors affecting the decision include:

(i)   It is assumed that the planes are identical whether leased or purchased.

(ii)   It is assumed that there will be no restrictions put on fittings, conversions or upgrades to the aircraft if they are leased (eg refitting of passenger seats).

(iii)   It may be more difficult to break the lease early than to sell the planes if business suffers a downturn. On the other hand if the planes are kept for the full 5 years, leasing avoids the risk of a drop in residual value.

(iv)   Purchasing becomes a progressively better option the longer the planes can be kept in service beyond 5 years.

Recommendation

In expected value terms, leasing is cheaper than purchasing. Assuming the planes will be replaced after 5 years, no earlier and no later, leasing is likely to be the better choice of finance, as it avoids the significant risk attached to residual value. If the period of use is uncertain, then purchasing may still be a better option.

(ii)   ## Wet lease

With an operating lease the lessee (V) does not receive the rights and benefits of ownership of the aircraft.

Advantages of the wet lease

(1)   The existing of the break clause in the contract allows V to terminate the contract after 3 years if the aircraft are no longer required or the project is deemed to not be worthwhile any longer.

(2)   Unlike the other acquisition methods, the lessor will be responsible for servicing and maintaining the aircraft, which could be relatively expensive given the age of the aircraft.

(3)   V does not have to worry about recruiting crew members for the aircraft where they may lack the experience to know which skills they are looking for.

(4)   V is protected by rising fuel costs, because these are included in the cost of the lease.

Disadvantages of the wet lease

The main disadvantage is the cost, which is likely to be significantly more expensive than the other forms of finance discussed.

Due to the uncertainty around the potential success of this venture, the wet lease is recommended as it carries less risk than either of the other options available. However, it should be noted that the full cost of this option must be known before any decision is taken.

Section C

(c) Post-completion audit

A post-completion audit compares the actual cash flows (inwards and outwards) of a project after it has reached the end of its life with the estimated cash inflows and outflows that were used in the original investment appraisal process. It is similar to carrying out variance analysis and the manager responsible for the project should be required to explain any significant variations from the estimated figures. It is used to aid the control process and lessons learned from the post-completion audit of a project can be fed into the next investment appraisal process.

An essential feature of a post-completion audit is the proper completion of an investment proposal, which should have clearly identified objectives that are ideally measurable. If V does not do this in advance then a post-completion audit is of limited value as there will be nothing to compare the actual results to.

As far as V is concerned, the main benefits from a post-completion audit include the following:

(i)   The chance to evaluate the person in overall charge of the project – were their cash flow estimates accurate or significantly different from reality? Have they performed well? How efficient have they been in the management of the project?

(ii) An opportunity to identify any problems in the forecasting techniques used. This information can be used to improve these techniques for the appraisal of future investments.

(iii) An opportunity to investigate any significant deviations from estimates and the reasons for these deviations. The determination of potential causes can be useful when estimating future cash flows.

The main limitations of a post-completion audit include the following:

(i)   Project managers may feel post-completion audits will be used to apportion 'blame' rather than for 'learning' purposes. They may try to claim credit for favourable results over which they had no influence whilst blaming external factors for adverse results that they could have prevented.

(ii) Post-completion audits can be expensive to undertake and as such may not be carried out. V may regard the aircraft purchasing investment as one that is unlikely to repeated very often and therefore fail to see any benefits from carrying out such an expensive process as any lessons learned will have little or no value for the future.

Conclusion

The post-completion audit does not seem to offer any significant value to V for the acquisition of the aircraft and therefore there it cannot be recommended. In addition, there are limited future cash flow estimates in this appraisal and as such it would not be appropriate to perform a post-completion audit.

In general, however, if there are major investment projects that are likely to be repeated, such as construction of specialised holiday resorts, then post-completion audits would provide valuable insight and lessons for V.

If you have any questions about the contents of this report, please do not hesitate to contact me.

(d) Benefits and problems of financing assets in the same currency as their purchase

If an asset generates income in a foreign currency, it is advantageous to finance its acquisition in the same currency. In this way, if the foreign currency depreciates, the loss in income is offset by lower financing costs.

Existence of long-term currency risk

However, if, as in the case of V, the aircraft are purchased and financed in a foreign currency but used to generate *home* currency income or savings, there is a long-term currency risk over the period of the finance. For example, if V negotiates a euro-denominated lease and the euro then strengthens by 10%, the costs of acquiring the asset will rise by 10% whereas the benefits of owning it in SK will be unchanged. This factor significantly reduces the attractiveness of V's euro lease.

Of course, if the euro weakened, the company would make exchange gains on its finance. On balance, however, investors are risk averse and tend to fear exchange losses more than they welcome the chance of exchange gains.

Significance of interest rate parity

A loan raised in a foreign currency sometimes carries a lower interest rate than a home currency loan. This is true in the example, where euro interest rates are 2% per annum lower than SK interest rates. However, the principle of interest rate parity suggests that the foreign currency (the Euro) will strengthen to compensate for this, resulting in an increased home currency value of loan or lease repayments.

Appendices

Appendix 1 – NPV of lease payments

The PV of the lease payments after tax relief, at 6% and 7%, is shown below. The lease is assumed to be an operating lease because the lessor retains the risk of loss on the residual value of the aircraft.

Time	0	1	2	3	4	5
lease	-1,050.0	-1,050.0	-1,050.0	-1,050.0	-1,050.0	
tax saved		315.0	315.0	315.0	315.0	315.0
NET	-1,050.0	-735.0	-735.0	-735.0	-735.0	315.0
Df 6%	1.000	0.943	0.890	0.840	0.792	0.747
PV	-1,050.0	-693.1	-654.2	-617.4	-582.1	235.3
NPV	**-3,361.5**					
Df 7%	1.000	0.935	0.874	0.817	0.764	0.714
PV	-1,050.0	-687.2	-641.7	-599.8	-560.8	224.6
NPV	**-3,314.9**					

Alternative format

	Year	SK$'000	6% factors	PV SK$'000	7% factors	PV SK$'000
Lease payments	0–4	(1,050)	4.467*	(4,690.4)	4.385*	(4,604.3)
Tax relief	1–5	315	4.212	1,326.8	4.100	1,291.5
				(3,363.6)		(3,312.8)

* $AF_{0-4} = AF_{1-5} / AF_1$

Note: Differences are due to rounding

Appendix 2 – NPV of purchase option

The planes cost SK$7m and their residual value is estimated as SK$3.5m. If they are bought, the tax savings from capital allowances will be as computed below. It is assumed that a balancing charge is made in year 5 because the assets are depreciated below their residual value.

Year	Value at start of year SK$'000	20% writing down Allowance SK$'000	30% tax saved SK$'000
1	7,000	1,400	420.0
2	5,600	1,120	336.0
3	4,480	896	268.8
4	3,584	716.8	215.0
5	2,867.2	(632.8)	(189.8)

The PV of purchasing the planes can then be estimated at 6% and 7%.

SK$000s

Time	0	1	2	3	4	5	6
outlay	-7,000.0						
WDA tax saved			420.0	336.0	268.8	215.0	-189.8
scrap						3500.0	
NET	-7,000.0	0.0	420.0	336.0	268.8	3715.0	-189.8
df 6%	1.000	0.943	0.890	0.840	0.792	0.747	0.705
PV	-7,000.0	0.0	373.8	282.2	212.9	2775.1	-133.8
NPV	**-3,489.8**						
df 7%	1.000	0.935	0.873	0.816	0.763	0.713	0.666
PV	-7,000.0	0.0	366.7	274.2	205.1	2648.8	-126.4
NPV	**-3,631.6**						

Alternative format

(Under this format there is one calculation that shows benefit of leasing over purchasing)

SK$000s

Time	0	1	2	3	4	5	6
lease	-1,050.0	-1050.0	-1050.0	-1050.0	-1050.0		
tax saved		315.0	315.0	315.0	315.0	315.0	
save outlay	7,000.0						
lost WDA			-420.0	-336.0	-268.8	-215.0	189.8
lost scrap						-3,500.0	
NET	5,950.0	-735.0	-1,155.0	-1,071.0	-1,003.8	-3,400.0	189.8
df 6%	1.000	0.943	0.890	0.840	0.792	0.747	0.705
PV	5,950.0	-693.1	-1,028.0	-899.6	-795.0	-2,539.8	133.8
NPV	**128.3**						
NET	5,950.0	-735.0	-1,155.0	-1,071.0	-1,003.8	-3,400.0	189.8
df 7%	1.000	0.935	0.873	0.816	0.763	0.713	0.666
PV	5,950.0	-687.2	-1,008.3	-873.9	-765.9	-2,424.2	126.4
NPV	**316.9**	(Difference due to rounding)					

Appendix 3 – Sensitivity to residual value

NPV of benefits of leasing

Year	0	1	2	3	4	5	6
	SK$'000	SK$'000	SK$'000	SK$'000	SK$'000	SK$'000	SK$'000
Lease payments	(1,050)	(1,050)	(1,050)	(1,050)	(1,050)		
Tax relief		315	315	315	315	315	
Purchase cost saved	7,000						
Residual value lost						(3,500)	
Tax allowances lost			(420.0)	(336.0)	(268.8)	(215.0)	189.8
Net cash flow	5,950	(735)	(1,155.0)	(1,071.0)	(1,003.8)	(3,400.0)	189.8
Discount factor 6.7% (W1)	1.000	0.937	0.878	0.823	0.772	0.723	0.678
PV	5,950	(688.7)	(1,014.1)	(881.4)	(774.9)	(2,458.2)	128.7
NPV	261.4						

Workings

(1)   Discount factors: Year 1 $\dfrac{1}{1.067} = 0.937$

Year 2 $\dfrac{1}{(1.067)^2} = 0.878$

Year 3 $\dfrac{1}{(1.067)^3} = 0.823$

Year 4 $\dfrac{1}{(1.067)^4} = 0.772$

Year 5 $\dfrac{1}{(1.067)^5} = 0.723$

Year 6 $\dfrac{1}{(1.067)^6} = 0.678$

Alternative format

If the previous alternative format has been used the net cash flow figures can be taken from those workings.

SK$000s

Time	0	1	2	3	4	5	6
from part (ii)	5,950.0	-735.0	-1,155.0	-1,071.0	-1,003.8	-3,400.0	189.8
df 6.7%	1.000	0.937	0.878	0.823	0.772	0.723	0.678
PV	5,950.0	-688.7	-1,014.1	-881.4	-774.9	-2,458.2	128.7
NPV	**261.4**						

The PV of the residual value of the aeroplanes $= SK\$3.5m \times \dfrac{1}{1.067^5} = 3.5m \times 0.723$

$= \$2,530,500$

The sensitivity of the calculation to changes in the residual value $= \dfrac{261,400}{2,530,500} = 10.3\%$

Question 9

Marking scheme

Note: There are a wide range of possible answers to this question. Any relevant, sensible points should get credit, even if they are not on the model answer or marking scheme.

Marks

Requirement (a)
Part (i) One mark per risk. Issues may include:
New venture – no track record
Competition – are others doing it better/worse?
Personal crusade
Investment required?
Profitable? Lots of elements to cost up
Costs of tickets to match premium status?
Revenues sustainable after Olympics?
Attraction of celebrities – trustworthy? Likeable? Available?
Insurance risks for guides?
Timescales and ticket availability?
Capacity – travel, accommodation etc.?
Current V IT system able to cope?
Cancellation policy if event does not go ahead?
Branch staff competent to sell this product?
Adverse impact on existing "Adventure" or "Prestige" holidays?
FOREX risks of new destinations?
MAXIMUM FOR REQUIREMENT **12**

Part (ii) Two marks per control:
Market research – Demand? Pricing? Impact on rest of V? Viable? Competitors?
Headhunt staff from competitors
Training
NPV to establish revenues, costs and sensitivities
Relationship with ticket sellers to guarantee access to events/"talent wranglers" for guides
Review IT system for capacity/flexibility
Pilot scheme to test the market
MAXIMUM FOR REQUIREMENT **8**

Requirement (b)
One mark per reasonable point. Issues may include:
Part (i) Information Systems – what do they want to do?
System needs to be automated, plus allows integration of new products with existing platforms
Links in real-time will speed up bookings and enhance reputation
Bookings recorded only once – no risk of loss or duplication of data or funds
Money easier to record
Information for accounting, decision-making and board reporting is easier to produce and consistent
MAXIMUM FOR REQUIREMENT **5**

Part (ii) Information Technology – how do they want to do it?
Branches need to use online system for consistency
Online system needs to connect to hotels and airlines
Sales system integrated with website and ledgers
EFTPOS consistency with website to match receipts to ledgers (network security critical)
Exec Info System (EIS) and Management Info System (MIS)
MAXIMUM FOR REQUIREMENT **5**

Part (iii) Information Management – who is going to be using it?
Branch staff
Head office booking staff
Customers
Accountancy staff
Board
MAXIMUM FOR REQUIREMENT   <u>5</u>

Requirement (c)
<u>Up to two marks per reasonable point. Points may include:</u>
Part (i) Quantitative measures
Isolate revenues and costs, including overheads
Margins/Contribution
Profitability by trip, customer or customer type
Cost drivers
Porter's Value Chain
MAXIMUM FOR REQUIREMENT   <u>8</u>

Part (ii) Qualitative measures
Balanced Scorecard
Loss-leaders
Churn
Identification of profitable customers
Quality control costs
Incentives
MAXIMUM FOR REQUIREMENT   <u>7</u>

TOTAL FOR QUESTION   <u>50</u>

Suggested solution

(a) (i) New venture – no track record

Introducing the "Events" range presents a substantial risk to V as it is a **new range** for V. Without first hand knowledge of this sector of the travel market, there is a very real risk that **mistakes** will be made that could be **costly** in many different ways. Although customers obtain the best tickets for events, their experience may be undermined by sub-standard accommodation, for example. If initial holidays offer a poor experience, and this is widely disseminated on-line, it may seriously damage V's reputation and undermine the viability of this range.

Competition – are others doing it better/worse?

The Executive Chairman's decision to introduce this product range seems to be based on his **emotions** rather than any **commercial analysis** of **gaps** in the market. There may be other more profitable and better established players in this market (such as Mike Burton) that V will have to compete with if this new product range is going to be a success.

Personal crusade

The fact that the Executive Chairman sees this as his legacy also presents risk. It may **discourage** board members from examining the proposals critically and could become a **financial burden** that affects **future investors** from associating with V.

Investment required

Any new product is going to require **new funds** that are either diverted from existing budgets or have to come from distributable earnings. Existing products may offer better prospects for delivering value. The company's **cost of capital** may also be affected by this range, making future projects inherently more expensive.

Profitability/Complexity

Each of the likely products in the new "Events" range will require a number of **different elements** to create the type of experience that the Executive Chairman has in mind – travel, accommodation, transfers, tickets, guides etc. – some of which may be difficult to **predict accurately in cost terms**. **Pricing** may be problematic as well as profitability assessment.

Costs of tickets to match premium status

Matching the premium nature of the product with access to events of a similar standard may require **more cost** than V has budgeted for, adding to the profit pressures on this new product.

Revenues sustainable after Olympics

It is understandable that the **"feel-good" factor** surrounding London 2012 will have generated substantial demand for sporting events in general. Once this **subsides**, there is a risk that **demand will drop**, adding further **pressure on prices** for the "Events" range which could adversely affect profits.

Attraction of celebrities

A central part of the "Events" range is the use of celebrities and sports stars to act as guides in order to attract customers to purchase such holidays. There is a risk that such people **may not be used to this kind of work** and **will not fulfil their commitments**. There is also a risk that some guides **may not attract enough customers** as it is unusual to have stars with universal popularity. The most appealing stars may already be committed to competitors or be prohibitively expensive to use. There may even be risk that V is **unable to attract the right kind of sports stars or celebrities** for their products.

Insurance risks for guides

As well as the risks to its customers and employees, V would also have to take steps to protect its high-profile guides on each "Events" tour. Such insurance costs may be prohibitive and could even **invalidate existing insurance arrangements.** Security and other costs (such as controlling paparazzi-style photographers) may also increase cost pressures on the product.

Timescales and ticket availability

Given the short timescales that the Executive Chairman has indicated, there is a risk that products will be **rushed** onto the market and may not be of **sufficient quality** to attract enough customers. Many sports-based holidays are **booked years in advance to guarantee tickets and accommodation** for specific events. V may already be coming to market too late for events such as Rio 2016.

Capacity

V evidently has capacity from its existing connections in the travel market, but it is unclear whether or not it can **expand** its **accommodation** and **other requirements** easily for this new product range.

Current V IT system

Given the Operations Director has already indicated that the existing IT systems at V may not be able to cope with any expansion, it is likely that the "Events" range will put **pressure** on the company's **information infrastructure,** which may have an **adverse impact** on the rest of its **products** and **branches.**

Cancellation policy if event does not go ahead

It is infrequent that a sporting or cultural event does not take place. However, for some sporting events such as the football World Cup, teams are knocked out in the qualifying stages and do not participate in the final tournament. Selling event tickets to fans whose teams have not been eligible to participate could affect profits via **insurance** or **reduced sales demand.**

Branch staff competent to sell this product

V's branch staff are supposed to make sure they are **familiar with products** by reading updates. A **new range** offering **complex products** in a **specialist market** presents a significant challenge that V should ensure all staff are prepared for, as any **initial failure** is likely to **reduce consumer demand** for the "Events" range.

Adverse impact on existing "Adventure" or "Prestige Travel" holidays

It is possible that in a market where consumers are struggling to afford products and can only take so much holiday in a year, introducing the "Events" range may simply **divert current V customers from V's existing products**, not adding to V's profits very much. It is possible that V may attract new customers but given its **limited approach to customer relationship marketing** and the **speed** of introducing this new product range, it may be **luck** rather than **judgement** that would see the attraction of net new customers.

FOREX risks of new destinations

It seems likely that V will deal with **new destinations** when arranging "Events" products. These could introduce **short-term transaction risks** for bookings as well as **translation risks** if any investment is required overseas. **Longer term economic risks** may also occur as currencies ebb and flow with the SK$, assuming the product range is successful enough to last this long.

(ii) **Market research (including competition)**

The most important thing for V to undertake is **market research** to determine the **demand** for such products and the likely costs of **supply. Pricing** strategy can then be devised in order to clarify the **premium nature** of the product. The potential **impact** on the rest of V should be considered as part of this research to ensure that there is no net loss of customers. Overall, market research will establish the **viability** of the "Events" range **beyond the emotive reasons** for doing it that are quoted by the Executive Chairman.

Part of the market research done by V will inevitably focus on who is already delivering **similar products** and **how they do it** (eg Virgin has a strategy based on either filling gaps in a particular market or doing a better job than those already present). This will help with **positioning** the product for maximum effect. It may also highlight that there is **no expansion opportunity** and so V should either **withdraw** its interest or look to either **acquire an existing provider** or enter some form of **joint venture.**

Headhunt staff from competitors

Given its **lack of experience** in this market, the introduction of the new product range may be easier for V with experienced staff involved, so it may decide to **head-hunt employees** from competitors who have the right kind of experience. This could start **at the very top** (such as Marks and Spencer appointing former Morrisons Chief Executive Marc Bolland to enhance its food business) and cascade right down through **management** to **sales staff** familiar with marketing such products, although V could complete a **skills audit** of its staff to establish if anyone has experience of this kind product in the short term.

Training

V needs to reconsider its approach to **training staff** not just in new products, but also in existing products. Issuing updates that staff may not read properly will not guarantee that customers receive the knowledgeable service that they require. Formal training courses will certainly be needed on major new products such as the "Events" range.

NPV

Once V is happy **in broad terms** that it has decided to pursue an apparently viable business opportunity, it will need to consider a **more detailed analysis** to establish **revenues**, **costs** and **sensitivities**, taking the **cost of capital** and **other key assumptions** into account. Adopting a net present value (NPV) approach will help reinforce the value-generating nature of this opportunity.

Relationship with ticket sellers/"talent wranglers"

Key to the success of the "Events" range is the company being able to **guarantee access** to the actual **events themselves**, so developing relationships with organisations who can supply tickets (such as Ticketmaster) will be essential unless V is prepared to either **pay more than necessary** or accept tickets of a **lower quality** than their product range implies.

Given the importance of **guides** to this new product range, V will also need to consider how to develop a reputation that **attracts top celebrities** and **sports stars** to its products. This may require the **appointment** of **staff** who can deal with **potential guides** and their **business partners** in order to arrange their involvement with specific products in a way that attracts, rewards and retains guides.

Review IT system for capacity/flexibility

V will need to undertake **stress tests** of its IT infrastructure to see if it can cope with the **introduction** of these new products. Individual **revenues will need recording** and **costs identifying** in order to establish early indicators of the **viability** of the range, and the system will need to ensure that it can cope with the **extra volumes of data** to be processed.

Pilot scheme to test the market

Organisations sometimes **test new products** with a small pilot scheme before rolling them out wholesale (such as **limited edition grocery products**) as a way of **ironing out problems**, **testing demand** and getting **better feedback than a focus group**. V could consider organising a limited number of "Events" products as pilots and avoiding initially the highest-profile events such as sports World Cups.

(b) (i) Information Systems – what do they want to do?

The first element of any information strategy is to ask **what it is the organisation wants to be able to do**. From the unseen information presented above, overwhelmingly, V needs a system that is **much more automated and less dependent on human intervention** for success.

The number of times that data is processed **manually** leaves V open to **data loss** and **processing error**. V should be looking to introduce a system that requires a **single data entry** for each item of sales revenue or cost which then **updates**, **processes** and **reports automatically**.

Adopting such a system will assist with the integration of **new products** with existing platforms, especially if the specification for V's new system identifies the need for it to be **"future-proofed"**. Similarly, **links** between the branches, head office and suppliers (such as hotels and airlines) in **real-time** will speed up bookings and enhance V's reputation with its customers, so investment in external and internal network connections should be considered.

V needs to ensure that **cash receipts** can be still recorded and reconciled satisfactorily in the new system, although it may wish to consider **whether the receipt of cash and cheques is still viable** if customers continue to prefer using cards. Such changes to payment methods need to be **balanced** against the loss of customer goodwill if they are removed.

Finally, the information requirements for **accounting**, **decision-making** and **board reporting** need to be considered in any information system. V should ensure that it adopts a system which allows it to produce reliable and consistent information for all **internal** and **external reporting**.

(ii) **Information Technology – how do they want to do it?**

Once V has decided what it wants to do, it needs to consider **how it is going to do it**. This requires implementing the necessary **technology** (hardware, connections and software) to do the job required within the funds available.

Both branch-based and head office staff need **real-time access** to airline and hotel systems, as do customers using the V website. It seems logical that **V's online system should connect directly to hotels and airlines in real-time**, allowing **customers**, **branch** and **head office staff** to use this online system for consistency of booking information.

Once these systems are all integrated, the sales system can be integrated with the website and all the various accounting ledgers to ensure data is updated automatically whenever a booking is taken and a deposit received. This will deliver EFTPOS (electronic funds transfer at point of sale) consistency with the website to match receipts to ledgers also.

Understandably, all this integration will require a **robust network**, which should be designed with likely **traffic need**, adequate **security protocols** and **disaster recovery** procedures built in.

Finally, V needs to consider the various **reporting needs** within the company and build this functionality into the new systems. It is likely that an **Executive Information System** (EIS) and **Management Information System** (MIS) are necessary, but others may be required too.

(iii) **Information Management – who is going to be using it?**

As described in part (ii) the needs of both **branch staff** and **head office booking staff** will dictate the majority of **user need** and therefore the amount of training and investment required. Similarly, ensuring that **customers** have the right kind of access to holiday information (ie marketing) but can also make bookings will dictate the format, layout and style of the system.

It is worth noting that if V continues to **expand its online presence**, the need for **branch staff may diminish** to the extent that **priority** systems become the **customer-facing website**. V should monitor traffic so it ensures it is always matching demand with resource. This could also require greater externalising of customer information, making it more customer-facing, such as something like 'MyBalance' which shows customers a detailed breakdown of what their holiday includes, how much they owe and when they need to pay it.

Finally, the system should ensure that it meets the needs of staff in the **finance department** (for whom **detail** is key) and the **Boardroom** (where **flexibility** and **decision-making** are prioritised).

(c) (i) **Quantitative measures used to analyse our products**

It would seem from our initial analysis of V's products that we need to isolate both **revenues** and **costs** for **each product** that we sell. This will require the identification of accurate estimates of our **overheads** and sensible allocation across **cost centres**. It is currently unclear whether we can isolate costs **by resort** or whether it extends to **individual flights**, **hotels** and **transfer** invoices.

Once we have greater **visibility** of our costs and can **match** them with appropriate **revenue** figures, we can start to calculate **margins** for each of our products. Again, the depth of detail here will depend on how much data we can collect and **how far down we can drill into this detail**. **Profit margins** are relatively simple measures but we may wish to consider others such **return on capital employed** (ROCE) for areas of the business where specific capital has been invested. Calculating the **contribution**

earned by specific holidays where **fixed costs** have been paid out (such as block bookings of hotel rooms) is another area that could work here.

One area we need to clarify is whether it is more meaningful to calculate the **profitability by trip** or **by customer**, as certain products (eg "Package" holidays for families) might generate varying "per capita" costs per holidaymaker depending on their profile which may not be as **meaningful** to compare these against holidays which only adults would take.

On a related note, we must consider identifying **cost drivers** – activities such as fuel, food, drink, staff etc. – within our business instead of cost centres, as these are likely to be better at **identifying** exactly what activities within V incur cost.

Finally, **Porter's Value Chain** could be an approach that we might find useful in identifying where V generates **profit** from the **value perceived by our customers** being **greater than** the **costs required to create that value**. The value chain discusses **support activities** (such as HR) as well as **primary activities** (such as customer service and marketing) that might be analysed further to identify profitable parts of V's business.

(ii) **Qualitative factors that could support our quantitative analysis**

In addition to pure financial analysis, understanding the **intangible** nature of what delivers value for V is important. The **Balanced Scorecard** is one such approach but there are other more specific examples which V could explore:

- We need to understand the importance of the "**loss-leader**" holiday (losing money on the first holiday sold to a customer but attracting them back for future holidays) as a means of delivering **longer term profits** to V. It is important **not only to attract but then retain customers** as their needs change and offer them different holidays, drawing on customer goodwill and recommendation (eg "Adventure" when they are young, "Package" once they have a family, then "Prestige" once their children have grown up).

- Retail organisations such as mobile phone providers use a measure known as "**churn**" which doesn't just look at the **net position of revenue** in a given period, it analyses how many customers are **new**, how many are **existing** and how many have **left during that period** and attempts to understand why changes to each might have occurred. Overall, this will help V to understand the **profile** of its customers and increase the likelihood of retaining their business.

- As an aside to this, the **identification of profitable customers** will help us to prioritise how they are marketed and how V maintains products that meets their needs. Building good customer **feedback** into product development is crucial here.

- V must develop an approach to **quality control** that identifies the **costs** associated with ignoring quality in order to establish a break-even point when quality control costs cease to be an **investment** and start to simply become **costs**. As with the balanced scorecard, quality and feedback must be seen to go hand in hand at V.

- Finally, we must consider whether the **incentives** we offer to our staff are goal-congruent with financial success at V. Ideally, better visibility of the most profitable holidays will help us to design sales incentives which maximise the volumes sold, rather than rely on historic patterns of reward that may not be quite so scientific.

Question 10

Marking scheme

Requirement (a) (i)
For each risk explained – up to 1½ marks
Risks may include:
Failure of joint venture partner
Failure of the joint venture
Damage to reputation
Failure to diversify risk
Political instability
Piracy risk
Problems with ships
Compliance risk
Disaster risk
Operational gearing risk   Max 12

Requirement (a) (ii)
For each control recommended and justified – up to 2 marks
Controls could include:
Due diligence
Joint venture contract
Destination planning
Reliance on ships
Disaster risk
Compliance risk
Operational gearing   Max 12

Requirement (b) (i)
Up to 2 marks for each point evaluated. Answers should cover:
Reputation
Financial costs
Compliance
                                                            Max 6

Requirement (b) (ii)
Up to 2 marks per valid step suggested. Answers may include:

Initial vetting (including quality standards such as ISO 9001)
Onsite inspections
Customer feedback
Monitoring and reporting
Customer education   Max 8

Requirement (c)
Up to 2 marks for each valid point discussed. To score full marks, given the 'evaluate' requirement, the answer should consider any positive aspects, not just identify risks. Suggestions may cover:

Complementary products
Investment
Reputational risks
Market conditions   Max 6

Requirement (d)

For each valid point suggested, including:

Adverts	1
Accessibility	1
Booking process	1
Alterations	1
Training	1
Complaints handling	1
	Max 6

TOTAL FOR QUESTION   <u>50</u>

Suggested solution

(a) (i) The additional risks that V will face in entering a joint venture with Blues Cruise will include:

Failure of the joint venture partner

If Blues Cruise is in **financial difficulties** or becomes so, then it may enter liquidation and be unable to perform its obligations under the joint venture (JV) arrangement. Its share of the JV might then need to be sold to the highest bidder and the JV may well **collapse** in this situation.

Failure of joint venture

The JV will entail **sharing risks, rewards and attitudes**. For the venture to be successful in a situation of joint control, it is important that the two partners can **agree** an approach to running the venture. V has achieved high levels of customer satisfaction and personal service. Blues Cruise does not appear to have a similar attitude to maximising customer satisfaction, so when decisions are taken on matters like budgets for training, it will be likely to cause **conflict**. The fact that Blues Cruise is based in Norway may cause **language problems** and **cultural issues**, with different attitudes to employment conditions or service provision.

Damage to reputation

As a result of conflicting **customer satisfaction levels** and the different **culture** within Blues Cruise, association with them may adversely affect the reputation attached to the rest of V's products, meaning that it loses parts of its core business that the JV cannot match.

Failure to diversify risk

One of the risks a cruise provider faces is the state of the economy. If the economy is weak, consumers tend to avoid or **reduce expenditure on discretionary items like holidays**. This also applies to the type of products that V currently sells, so the JV will not help to diversify economic risk. The cruise business is also **seasonal** and therefore bears the same **cash flow risks**. It is equally exposed to the rising cost of **fuel** and other **economic risks** associated with currency fluctuations.

Political instability

The intention is to run cruises around Africa and the Indian Ocean. Large parts of Africa are still **unstable**, with the changes due to the **Arab Spring** leaving several countries in North Africa with new governments and unstable democracies. Although the ships will be at sea, it is normal to **visit ports** as part of the cruise and also to organise excursions. **Unrest** might therefore affect the passengers and crew.

Piracy risk

Somalia remains a centre for piracy and the Indian Ocean is **very dangerous**. If pirates boarded a liner and people were killed the reputational damage would be significant to both JV partners, and they could face substantial legal claims from survivors or relatives of dead passengers.

Problems with ships

It is unclear how many ships will be used for VB Cruises, but due to the capital cost involved it is unlikely that ships will be kept in reserve in case of **breakdowns**. This means a greater level of reliance than V currently has, since if a hotel is unavailable it is often possible to arrange for customers to stay at alternative hotels in the same location. If a ship breaks down and requires significant time in dock, there will be **no alternative** but to **cancel holidays** and **refund deposits**.

Compliance risk

Although V already has to comply with various rules and laws as part of the travel industry, VB Cruises will need to comply with an **additional set of regulations** around **maintenance of seaworthy ships**, **health and safety on board**, appropriate levels of correctly **qualified crew** and **rules of navigation**. While Blues Cruise already has this knowledge, it will make V very reliant on its partner, whose attitude to ethics may not be the same as V's.

Disaster risk

Even worse than a breakdown would be a ship sinking. The **Costa Concordia** hitting rocks off the coast of Italy in January 2012 demonstrated that although these events are rare, they do happen (in fact there have been 30 reported groundings of liners since 2008, some of which resulted in ships sinking). The impact of the **weather** will also be potentially more significant, as it could prevent a ship from leaving port or require a change of route.

Operational gearing risk

Currently V sells holidays but pays hotels to provide accommodation. Although there is a risk of booking more rooms than can be sold, it is possible to cancel with relatively small penalties. VB Cruises will have all the **fixed costs** of owning and running a fleet of ships, regardless of **occupancy rates**. Fixed costs will include depreciation and mooring costs when in port and fuel costs when at sea.

(ii)   Controls to mitigate the risks identified above could include:

Due diligence

Before agreeing to the joint venture, V should appoint a professional services firm to perform due diligence on Blues Cruise. The due diligence will need to cover any aspects of the business relevant to the joint venture. These would include **financial stability**, adherence to **laws and regulations**, the nature and quality of **IT systems** in use and the company's **safety record**.

Joint venture contract

To avoid subsequent **misunderstanding** and **conflict** it is critical that experienced lawyers are involved in drafting a contract that clarifies the objectives and operation of the joint venture. The **split** of **profit** and **capital contributions** must be stated along with the **decision making process** and **accountability** in all events. There should be terms dealing with what happens should one party **fail to perform its obligations** and a clear process for **terminating** the joint venture.

Destination planning

It is not possible to **eliminate** the risk of a cruise ship arriving in a country as civil war breaks out. However, **targeting** countries that have a reasonable history of stability will reduce the risk. **Monitoring of governmental advice** (similar to the UK's Foreign and Commonwealth Office Travel Advice) will enable **rapid identification** of potential problems. VB Cruises will need a **contingency plan** to use in the event of unforeseen **civil disturbance**.

Reliance on ships

This will be partly controlled by ensuring that necessary **maintenance** is **planned** and then **performed** appropriately. This will require sufficient resource allocation and, again, reliance on Blues Cruise's expertise. To deal with **unexpected ship unavailability**, VB Cruises will need **terms** and **conditions** in their **contracts with customers**. These should include the ability to offer **alternative cruises or holidays** via V, to reduce the incidence of refunds. It may also be possible to **insure** against this risk.

Disaster risk

This should be controlled via **insurance** of all of the ships. However, the insurance **premium** will be expensive unless VB can demonstrate it has **controls** in place to reduce the chance of ships being lost. These controls would include use of **competent staff** and **up to date technology** (eg satellite navigation and forward looking 3D sonar equipment). While this will help, the staff are still required to act **diligently**, which appeared to be the problem in the case of the Costa Concordia.

Compliance risk

The main **regulatory body** covering shipping is the International Maritime Organisation, sponsored by the UN. To ensure compliance it will be necessary to know what the **rules** are. Blues Cruise should have this knowledge and already have **controls to ensure adherence**. However, V will need to be satisfied these controls are **adequate**. The controls should cover **monitoring changes to the rules**, **training** of staff in order that they can follow the rules (with updates as required) and a **monitoring procedure** via **internal audit** or a **dedicated compliance department**. There should be regular **inspections** of ships to ensure that they are **seaworthy** and have the **necessary safety equipment** (lifeboats etc).

Operational gearing

In order to maximise **utilisation** of the ships, the **pricing structure** will need to be flexible, with **late deals** available to fill empty cabins. This will require a system that provides **up-to-date booking information** and **regular monitoring** by an appropriate level of management.

(b) (i) The risks faced by V arising out of the issues at Hotel Barbados include:

Reputational damage

The reputational damage will be two-fold. Firstly V will lose the **repeat business** from the dissatisfied customers, who will blame V for sending them to a sub-standard hotel, irrespective of the Operations Director's view. Secondly the fact that the action group is being supported by a consumer organisation means this story may achieve a **high profile** in the media, causing a **loss of other potential customers**. The use of social media and websites like 'Tripadvisor' mean that bad news spreads fast.

Financial costs

In order to placate the action group V may have to offer **compensation**. Since the customer contract was with V, not the hotel, it will be for V to compensate customers. If not, a **legal case** could follow, resulting in higher compensation costs and legal costs as well. It will then be for V to try to recover the costs from Val-u, incurring further legal costs.

The risks faced by Val-u include:

Reputational damage

If the hotel chain is known for **low health and safety standards**, holiday companies like V will **stop using it**. This would leave it with a serious **shortfall of revenue**, as the bulk of its customers would come via travel companies rather than direct booking. Even with customers booking directly, they are likely to read reviews of the hotel before booking and **bad reviews will cost the chain business**.

Compliance costs

The Operations Director is **right** to say that V can't be responsible for poor safety standards at a hotel. That **duty** lies with the **hotel management**, and it will be the **hotel chain** that gets **fined** by the relevant regulatory body. However, it is not necessarily the case when using hotels abroad that the regulatory **standards** of the **country** where the hotel is located are **as high as European standards** and therefore what a citizen of SK might regard as a breach of health and safety **wouldn't necessarily result in the hotel getting fined**.

It is also important to **distinguish** between the three issues mentioned. **Faulty fire prevention** and **evacuation procedures** are definitely something the hotel should be accountable for. It is harder to prove Val-u is at fault with regard to the **stomach upsets**. While they are probably due to **incorrect handling of food** in the hot climate, **tests** are rarely done at the time to establish the **cause** of the outbreak. A man **drowning** in a pool due to a heart attack is unfortunate, but hotel pools are often **unsupervised**, especially late at night when this accident occurred, so it is harder to allocate blame to the hotel unless they had **claimed to always supervise swimming pools**.

(ii) The steps V should take to mitigate the risks of substandard hotel performance would include:

Initial vetting

This would require an **audit** of the hotel chain's **health and safety standards**. The chain should have **written procedures** covering health and safety, and evidence that management **monitor** adherence to the standards. The standards themselves should be adequate to satisfy SK's health and safety requirements, not just local ones. Thomas Cook, for instance, require suppliers to satisfy **ISO 9001**. However, once a company has been placed on an **approved supplier list** it is important that it is still **monitored**. For instance, the Val-u chain has been acquired by a **hedge fund** so it is possible that the hedge fund has embarked on a **cost cutting programme** that may be at the root of the health and safety problems, so the **original assessment** of Val-u may be **out of date**.

On site inspections

V has a **representative** in each location. One of their **tasks** should be to perform **health and safety assessments** on a regular basis. This would ensure that **sufficient fire drills** were taking place and sufficient **fire prevention measures** were in place, such as testing of electrical equipment. They could check that the **food preparation areas and pools are maintained** to an appropriate standard of **cleanliness**, since this could also be a cause of the stomach upsets. These inspections should be supplemented by more rigorous visits by a **dedicated health and safety team**, with **more specialised knowledge and equipment**. They could test **water quality**, **food handling procedures** and **food storage temperatures**.

Customer feedback

Rather than waiting for letters of complaint, V should **actively seek feedback on customer experience**. Where problems are **identified**, a health and safety team should be sent to **investigate** and resolve the issue promptly. The chain should then be **targeted** for more **regular inspections** to ensure the hotel chain or specific hotel has dealt with the issue.

Monitoring and reporting

Senior management should collect **statistics** relating to health and safety and publicise them externally. Thomas Cook, for instance, publishes **health and safety information** in its **sustainability report**. The statistics are **monitored** under the headings of **balcony related**, **pool related**, **transport related** and **other**. By declaring this information externally it provides **additional focus** to management to ensure the holiday locations are as **safe** as possible.

Customer education

As a preventative measure, V should be providing **good advice to customers** such as to only drink **bottled water** and to **avoid ice cubes** in drinks. This will **reduce** the incidence of customers getting ill.

(c) The Executive Chairman is right to worry about the **utilisation** of branches as more and more holiday booking is done online, and often direct with the hotel or airline. Maintaining a **branch network** is **expensive** and many travel companies have been closing branches. However, it would be **simplistic** to say that the **commission** is **risk free**.

BPP
LEARNING MEDIA

Complementary products

Since V also sells holidays it is possible that selling a competitor holiday in the branch will be **at the expense of one of V's own holidays**. This would probably have provided a **bigger margin** than V will earn from the **commission** and could potentially leave V with a **surplus** of hotel rooms. This could be mitigated by being **selective** in which holiday companies they sell on behalf of (eg companies that offer holidays to **different locations** or **specialist holidays** that V does not offer). Doing this would increase the **range** of customer profiles that V could service, which would lead to **incremental revenue**.

Investment

The idea would require **costs** to be incurred which the commission revenues may not cover. The staff would need to be **trained** so they had **sufficient product knowledge** of these other products (although this is not an area V seems to prioritise anyway). The company's **IT infrastructure** will probably require investment in order to be able to **link** to competitor systems. This would also create **security risks** as it would be potentially possible for that **competitor** to gain **access** to V's **confidential information**. Also, if the other company's security was weak, it could expose V's system to **hacking** or **viruses**. It would also be important that the other companies' systems worked **quickly** and **accurately** or the service in the branches would be **slow** and the incorrect holiday booking information might be recorded.

Reputational risks

If V sells a customer a holiday provided by a **competitor** and the customer has a **bad holiday**, the customer will be **unlikely to buy holidays from V in the future**, even though V is **not responsible** for the actual holiday experience. Customers view travel agents as a source of **advice** and will consider they were given **bad advice** by V.

Market conditions

The **motivation** for the idea is apparently to utilise **spare capacity** in the branches as bookings go online. However, market conditions would affect all travel agents just as much as V and there is a danger that a lot of management time and money goes into setting up a business that produces **little commission** as holiday makers book direct with suppliers anyway. Although customers appear to value V's excellent customer service, they may **use the branches for advice only** and then **book direct** to save money.

(d)   The following tests would be recommended:

Adverts

Internal Audit (IA) should review **marketing literature** for evidence of **breaches of regulations**. **Prices** quoted could be checked to **authorised price lists** and **customer sales values**. Details of holidays could be checked for **accuracy** against the **adverts**. **Complaints files** should be reviewed for evidence of customers suggesting the **brochure details did not match the actual hotel provided** or complaining about **lack of clarity regarding prices**.

Accessibility

The accessibility of branches can be checked by **site visits**. Ramp or lift access should be available, branch counters should be an appropriate height and staff should display **awareness** of equality issues. IA should check that **staff training** covers this issue.

Booking process

IA should, as part of site visits, **observe** the process of booking, although this is likely to be influenced by their presence so they may consider the use of "**mystery shoppers**" perhaps. There should be standard **documentation**, with **checklists** to ensure the customer has been **informed** of all **key aspects** of the holiday such as the need for **vaccinations** and **travel insurance**, and that they have been made aware of the **terms and conditions** attached to their booking. The customer should **sign** this document to **confirm** that all appropriate information has been provided. IA can select a **sample** of these to ensure the checklist has all the necessary checks on it to satisfy regulations, that the checklist has been correctly **completed** and that the customer has **signed** it.

Alterations to bookings

Since these are only allowed in **restricted circumstances**, IA should review a **sample** of bookings that were **amended** and ensure that the amendment was for a **valid reason**, such as **volcano eruption** or an **earthquake**. Where alterations were for valid reasons IA should check that **appropriate communication** took place with the customer and that the customer was offered an **appropriate** holiday alternative.

Training

V should provide all staff with training to ensure that they know the **correct procedures** for **advertising** and **processing bookings** in accordance with **regulations**. As well as the testing done during site visits, IA should audit the **training records** to ensure all staff have **received** appropriate and adequate training.

Complaints handling

Complaints handling will be subject to various deadlines eg **acknowledgement** of complaints with in a **specific time period**. The complaints file can therefore be used to select a **sample** of individual complaints which can then be **tracked** to ensure **each step was taken** within the **appropriate time frame**. IA can also check that **correct responses** were made at each step of the process eg no decisions to **reject valid complaints**.

Question 11

Marking scheme

Marks

Requirement (a)
1 mark per reasonable point. Limit to 8 marks if no points in favour, as discussion was required
For

Clear leadership – needed at time of change, consistent with culture, outsider may disrupt	Max 3
Problems of Chairman – learning curve, lack of time, credibility	Max 2

Against

Investor reaction – important if going public, require compliance with governance best practice, view Chief Executive with unfettered power as risky	Max 3
What new Chairman can provide – critical external perspective, relevant knowledge and skills, attracts new NEDs	Max 3
Demands of roles – difficult for one person to do both effectively, 2 people can focus on different areas	Max 2
Running board – separate Chairman promotes discussion, contribution from all board members, board development	Max 3
Accountability – need to ensure Chief Executive accountable to board, Chairman/Chief Executive otherwise difficult to control	Max 2
MAXIMUM FOR REQUIREMENT	**13**

Requirement (b)
Up to 2 marks for each recommendation (2 recommendations max per header).
Recommendations under each header should measure different aspects:
Financial
Customer
Learning and growth
Internal business processes

MAXIMUM FOR REQUIREMENT	**12**

Tutor's note. The balanced scorecard could also be examined in the E3 exam.

Requirement (c) (i)
1 mark per reasonable point
Ethics

Integrity – honesty issues, fair dealing with customers and internally	Max 2
Objectivity – staff unduly influenced by bonuses	Max 1
Professional behaviour – staff rule-breaking, management condoning	Max 1
Professional competence – staff error, lack of staff training	Max 2

Commercial

Legal penalties – fines, loss of revenue as can't offer insurance	Max 2
Customers – lost sales due to lost trust, potential impacts on all products, not just insurance	Max 2
Staff – demotivation of honest staff, costs of staff departing	Max 2
Investors – commercial impact of actions against V, concerned by culture of dishonesty/incompetence	Max 2
MAXIMUM FOR REQUIREMENT	**10**

Requirement (c) (ii)

1 mark per reasonable point

Board – clear message from board, one director oversees ethics	Max 2
Change code of ethics – counter problems found, ensure consistent with regulations	Max 2
Staff training – must be included in induction	Max 1
Training of existing staff – training needs analysis, must cover products and ethics	Max 2
Balanced scorecard – range of measures will promote better behaviour	Max 1
Disciplinary action – sanctions against staff and branch managers	Max 2
MAXIMUM FOR REQUIREMENT	6

Requirement (d)

1 mark per reasonable point

Hedging – different from hedging overseas payments, customers bear risks over time	Max 2
Exchange rates – dependent on commercial considerations, rates obtainable	Max 2
Other risks	
Impact on product portfolio, diversification	Max 2
Setting terms – need to keep up with changing exchange rates, assess optimum margin on each currency	Max 2
Product development – need to provide extra services, but does V have infrastructure	Max 2
Reputation risk – complex charging structures are unpopular, see in light of other threats to reputation, especially fuel surcharging	Max 2
MAXIMUM FOR REQUIREMENT	9

TOTAL FOR QUESTION	**50**

Suggested solution

(a) **Combining the roles**

Clear lead

Having the current Operations Director take the lead role means that V will have a **clear leadership position** at a forthcoming time of significant change. The new Executive Chairman will be able to give a clear lead on **strategic issues.** V is also used to having a single person in clear charge. The involvement of a separate Chairman may complicate board operations and lead to disagreement, particularly if the new Chairman comes from a different corporate culture.

Gaining knowledge

A non-executive Chairman from outside the travel industry will need time to gain knowledge and its products, but will have **constraints on how much time he or she can commit**, as the role is only part-time. This may result in the Chairman lacking credibility initially in board meetings and he or she may struggle to overcome this problem.

Separating the roles

Investor reaction

If V is to seek a listing in the foreseeable future, investors are unlikely to view the **combination of roles favourably.** They are likely to look adversely on the **failure to follow governance guidance** on the separation of roles. Other companies, such as Marks and Spencer, that have tried to explain their reasons for the same person doing both jobs have found that investors have not accepted their explanations. Investors may also feel that the new Executive Chairman at present lacks the credibility to be given unfettered power.

Outside experience

A Chairman from outside V should be able to step back and see the company from an **external perspective** and understand what aspects may need to develop and change. The Chairman may also be able to provide specific **knowledge and experience** that will assist V, for example experience of developing more formal governance structures. A Chairman with an **excellent external reputation** may also encourage the recruitment of other strong non-executive directors. V will have to consider the recruitment of further non-executives if it gains a listing and wishes to comply with government guidance.

Demands of both roles

The roles of Chairman and Chief Executive are both **demanding roles** in terms of the **time required and responsibilities.** As newly-appointed Chief Executive, the Operations Director will be on a **learning curve** in this role, and the learning process will be much more demanding if he takes on both roles. An experienced Chairman will be able to help him with this process. Splitting the roles will allow both office-holders to **concentrate on tasks** that will be very important in enhancing V's appeal to external investors. The Chief Executive will be able to concentrate on developing new strategies and products and matching resources available with the product expansion. The Chairman will be able to concentrate on developing new governance structures and building relations with new shareholders.

Ensuring discussion

Particularly at a time of major development for the company, it is important that plans are discussed and challenged before decisions are made. Having a separate Chairman to run the board and control its meetings will provide a more **effective forum for discussion** of the Chief Executive's plans for changing V. The Chairman can ensure **active engagement** in meetings by all members of the board, not just those who agree with the Chief Executive. The Chairman can also **facilitate board development** on both an individual basis and a team basis. V may be **more attractive to investors** if they perceive it is being run by a strong team rather than a dominant individual.

Accountability to the board

Splitting the roles emphasises that the Chairman carries the **authority of the whole board** whereas the Chief Executive has only the authority that is **delegated by the board**. The Chairman should be able therefore to hold the Chief Executive **accountable** to the board. Having the same person exercise both roles means that person has unfettered power and makes it less likely that the rest of the board can exercise effective control.

(b)   **Financial**

Growth in sales

Sales targets should remain a significant means of monitoring short-term performance, even if they are not the sole means used to determine reward. Quarterly sales reporting can be supplemented by **monthly reporting** for particularly busy months. As well as making **comparisons with the previous period**, management can also **compare figures for the equivalent period** in the previous year to take account of **seasonal variations** and with other branches.

Return on investment

Longer-term measures are also needed, partly to mitigate for any distortions in shorter-term measures and also because staff turnover is low and hence staff's performance needs to be viewed over the whole term which they are employed. In addition V is currently considering whether to **reduce its branch network** due to increases in the proportion of on-line sales, and hence needs to assess the return continuing to run branches will bring. Hence one or more **return on investment** figures should be calculated, with investment being measured in terms of staff employed or floor area.

Customer

Customer satisfaction

V has used its own surveys to monitor customer satisfaction and obtained a 99% satisfaction rating. However the rating and the criticisms made by the external consumer watchdog are likely to have greater credibility with the public and reflect badly on V generally, not just on the branches criticised. V therefore needs to **monitor external sources** for information about its customers' views and also **develop its own internal measures,** asking customers more specific questions in surveys and prompting responses by follow-up phone calls or emails.

Repeat bookings

V will retain customer details and should therefore assess over a period of time what proportion of customers make **multiple bookings** through V's branches. The fact that customers return will be an indication that they are satisfied with the service that they have been given. It also will provide valuable information to V about **customer preferences**. If a high proportion of customers return to branches, this indicates that they value the human contact branches provide as opposed to booking on-line. It also reflects the new Executive Chairman's desire to **focus on customer relationship marketing.**

Learning and growth

New products

If V is to develop new products, it needs to **monitor the return** from them and also **validate the training** that staff have been given. Hence the sales information provided by branches should detail **separately sales of new products**. Branches should also keep a record of staff training in new products. Management should review these records, firstly to see whether branches have **followed guidelines** in sending staff for training and secondly to **review changes in sales** after the training has taken place.

Customer handling

V also needs to respond to the criticisms about the **ways customers have been treated** and assess whether **initial training is adequate** or staff need periodic refresher training. A commonly-used way of assessing an important aspect of staff performance is to record, on a random basis, **phone calls**

between staff members and customers. **Qualitative feedback** can then be provided to individual staff members and aggregated for the branch as a whole to provide an indication of training needs.

Internal business processes

Queries received

Central management also ought to receive details of the **volume and subjects of queries** received after initial bookings have been made. These could indicate failure by staff to **make everything clear** when the holiday was booked. If the queries relate to the airline, hotel or insurance provider that customers will be using, they could indicate problems with these suppliers that V will need to address.

Discounts offered

Management ought to review the **level of discounts** being given by branch managers, as they could represent a failure to maximise revenues. The discounts given should be compared between branches and viewed over different products, but must be seen in the **context of sales generated.** A large number of discounts could be justified by a high volume of sales. Contrawise a poorly-performing branch offering few discounts could be being too conservative.

(c) (i) **Ethics**

Integrity

If staff are knowingly making false statements, such as buying travel insurance is compulsory, it clearly **breaches the principle of truthfulness**. It also breaches the principle of **fair dealing**, not only with customers who are being deceived, but internally as well. Staff's remuneration is being determined partly by the **amount of travel insurance sold** and staff who act honestly will lose out to staff who have deceived customers.

Objectivity

The advice staff give to customers may have been **influenced by the current bonus arrangements and not customer well-being**. Staff may have been tempted to sell inappropriate insurance to increase revenues and hence their own rewards.

Professional behaviour

Staff who have deliberately provided **misleading advice about products** have broken the rules of the financial services authority. Possibly also branch management has broken the authority's rules by condoning or ignoring evidence of staff malpractice.

Professional competence and due care

If staff have unwittingly given the wrong advice, this may suggest a **lack of care or mistakes** on their part. Again however management may also be responsible for not ensuring that competent staff have given advice. The current arrangements, that staff 'will become familiar with products as they gain experience', is an **inadequate method** of training them about their responsibilities under financial services legislation.

Commercial implications

Penalties

V may be liable to **legal penalties** imposed **by the financial services authority**. The authority may demand V expends resources training staff, or limits the branches and staff allowed to sell insurance. Ultimately the authority could **withdraw V's authorisation** to sell insurance. Not only would V lose the direct insurance revenues, it might adversely affect the revenues from its overall holiday packages, as they become less attractive to customers without the inclusion of insurance.

Customers

Adverse publicity about misselling insurance may impact upon **other sales**, if it means that customers question whether what they are being told by V's staff is accurate. The bad publicity could hit sales in other branches as well as the branches that have transgressed.

Staff

V's staff turnover is low, suggesting a culture of **loyalty from existing staff** and experience, which should result in a better service for customers. This could be undermined by the news about misselling. Staff that have followed the rules may be angry that they have been less well-rewarded compared with staff who have missold insurance. This could result in **good staff leaving**, perhaps going to work for competitors. Expenditure would then be required on recruiting and training new staff.

Investors

Potential investors may not be very worried if there are only isolated incidents of missold insurance or the consequences are not serious. They may be more concerned if V's **authorisation is withdrawn** or **misselling is widespread,** suggesting a poor corporate culture.

(ii) **Message from the board**

The Board should issue a message stressing V's commitment to ethical sales practice and that dishonest behaviour will not be tolerated. The board should appoint one of the directors as an **'ethics champion',** who should supervise the development of reporting channels for staff who are concerned about colleagues' behaviour to use.

Code of ethics

V should review its code of ethics and consider strengthening the parts that relate to **honest behaviour and customer service**. Possibly the code needs to contain clear prohibitions of **deliberate misselling. Needs of customers** should be stressed as being paramount. The board should also ensure the code is **consistent with the regulatory requirements** that V faces.

Training of new staff

The induction process for new staff needs to include sufficient training about **insurance products and legal requirements**. Its inclusion needs to be considered as part of a wider review of initial training, with more time being spent on briefing staff on products.

Training of existing staff

A **training needs analysis** also needs to be undertaken for existing staff. V should make sure that only staff who have received **sufficient training about insurance products** are authorised to offer insurance advice. Authorisation should be withdrawn until re-training takes place if staff are found to have made serious mistakes. V should also consider also consider whether all staff need **further ethics training.**

Balanced scorecard

By placing greater emphasis on **customer satisfaction, training and good internal processes**, the introduction of the balanced scorecard described above should assist in preventing poor behaviour and ensuring staff are adequately trained in future.

Disciplinary action

Disciplinary investigations should be undertaken against staff who are found to have missold insurance. If they appear to be guilty of **dishonesty or serious negligence**, dismissal should be considered. Sanctions should also be taken against **branch managers** whose staff are found to have missold insurance, with sanctions including ineligibility for bonus, demotion or dismissal depending on their culpability.

(d) **Director's queries**

Hedging

The position on supplier payments abroad will be determined by movements in exchange rates over time. Natural hedges for payments over time will be receipts in the same currency over the same time period. By contrast with the currency card, V's margins will be determined by the **rate it buys the currencies** and the rate it **sells the currencies on to customers** on their cards, together with any other fees. As these transactions will occur within a short time, V would not suffer significant exposure on these transactions. The customers will effectively **bear foreign exchange risk** on the balances that remain at the end of their holiday, since the exchange rate used to redeem this currency will be based on the current rate of the time of redemption and not the rate when they took the card out. If V was to bear this risk, this would mean that introducing greater uncertainties in foreign currency management, as V would bear any good or bad changes in market rates, and also perhaps find it difficult to predict amounts that would be redeemed at the end of customers' holidays.

Exchange rates used

How large the margins are on V's exchange dealings will depend on commercial considerations. One appeal of this type of card is that exchange rates tend to be more favourable than those offered at airport kiosks, so margins may need to be **low to appeal to customers**. As V is not a particularly large organisation, the terms on which it obtains its currency may not be very favourable. Another factor is that some of the cards are sold to customers who do not buy holidays from V. Arguably therefore they are partly a **low profit product**, designed to attract customers to V's branches, who can then be persuaded to buy other products.

Other risk issues

Product diversification risks

The cards can be seen as a means of **product diversification and hence risk management**. The demand for the cards is probably not strongly positively correlated with demands for V's holidays, since they can be used on any type of trip abroad or by overseas tourists coming to V's home country.

Risks relating to terms offered

V will need to ensure that rates offered on the cards **are continually changed**, in line with rate changes on foreign currency markets. If this is not done, V's margins may be reduced as actual rates move. Maximum profitability on the cards may also be difficult to gauge, because the optimum margins on different currencies may vary.

Risks relating to development of cards

At present it appears that the cards are issued once and cannot be topped-up subsequently, nor used other than at ATMs. Their sales will suffer if **other cards can be used more flexibly**. However if V is to allow top-ups, this may place a strain on existing IT systems and require **significant extra development.**

Reputation risk

V's reputation may suffer adversely because of the cards if its **charging structure is felt to be complex or unfair**. Even if it makes its charging structure clear, it will no doubt receive complaints that the charges are only shown in the small print. V may be particularly sensitive about threats to its reputation here, because of the recent criticisms over its level of service and insurance misselling. V's holiday customers may also suffer a supplementary charge on airline fuel which they perceive to be unfair.

Question 12

Marking scheme

Requirement (a) (i)

1 mark for each well-explained point.

Risks

Development: costs excessive, project delays

Legal obstacles

Economic risks affecting relative demand

Increased operating gearing

Compliance with local legislation

Employment of local staff: employment law, culture

Control systems: require development when already inadequate

Increased liability for compensation

Fall in property value

Reputation risk: high risk when opened, can't be mitigated by changing hotels

MAXIMUM FOR REQUIREMENT   <u>10</u>

Requirement (a) (ii)

1 mark for each well-explained point. NOTE that the question asked solely about the controls over the development process. No credit to be awarded for controls over the hotel once it starts operating:

Controls can include:

Use of local legal expertise

Use of local construction manager

Project team including senior staff

Tendering/reference checking

Contracts: timescale/costs/penalty and rectification clause

Regular/urgent reporting

Site inspections

Contingency planning

MAXIMUM FOR REQUIREMENT   <u>8</u>

Requirement (b) (i)

1 mark for each well-explained point

Cost of debt

Limited availability of funds

Debt capacity

Commitment to more fixed costs

Hedging by matching assets and liabilities

Hedging by matching income and expenditure

Repayment schedule of loans

MAXIMUM FOR REQUIREMENT   <u>7</u>

Requirement (b) (ii)

Use of SK$ throughout	Max 1
Initial outflow	Max 1
Interest annuity	Max 4
Exchange rates	Max 2
Repayment	<u>Max 1</u>
MAXIMUM FOR REQUIREMENT	<u>9</u>

Requirement (c)

1 mark for each well-explained risk or control discussed. Max 3 under each risk header

Risks can include:

Low demand: marketing and market research leading to differentiation

Financial losses due to cut-price deals from competitors: market intelligence, flexibility in discounting

Excessive consumption and costs: financial controls, use ways of limiting consumption such as buffets

Theft by staff: monitor inventory, limit access

MAXIMUM FOR REQUIREMENT <u>10</u>

Requirement (d)

1 mark for each well-explained point discussed:

Complaints/poor feedback

New staff

HR issues indicating discontent

Poor supervision

Results of analytical review

Inadequate/non-existent documentation

MAXIMUM FOR REQUIREMENT <u>6</u>

TOTAL FOR QUESTION <u>50</u>

Suggested solution

(a) (i) **Development risks**

There are a number of risks associated with the development. These include the builders failing to **complete the work** (due, for example, to bankruptcy), the work being **delayed**, the development **containing faults** and disputes arising with the builders about these and the development costing more than was originally budgeted.

Unfavourable conditions in country where hotel is being built

V may be a victim of **discrimination by local or national government,** for example being subject to onerous local regulations or subsidies being given to local businesses. V may also suffer **penalties** through ignorance of, and hence non-compliance with, local regulations.

Economic risks

V must consider the potential impact of its **home currency weakening** against the currency of the country in which the hotel is located, as has been predicted by the forecast. The economic impact will depend on whether V responds to currency movements by **increasing prices**. V will also be vulnerable to a **weakening of the currencies of countries in which it currently does not operate**. The weakening may mean **holidays** in these countries become **cheaper**, and demand therefore shifts towards them and away from the country in which the hotel is located.

Operating gearing risk

As V will be incurring hotel running costs that are not dependent on demand, a **greater proportion of its costs will be fixed** and its **operating gearing will rise**. There is therefore a risk of **much lower profits** if demand is not as predicted.

Compliance risks

Compliance risks are likely to be **increased** if V operates a hotel itself. V will be responsible for obtaining some evidence that the local hotels it uses have procedures in place to ensure compliance. However, with its own hotel, V will itself have to **develop and ensure implementation of control procedures** in areas such as food hygiene and health and safety. V may also suffer **penalties** through ignorance of, and hence non-compliance with, local regulations.

Staff risks

V will also face **increased complexities through employing staff** in a hotel rather than just using on-site representatives. Employment law requirements for different staff may be complex and V may face difficulties in **managing staff who are used to a different working culture.**

Control systems risks

V is already struggling with issues with its management accounting systems and information systems and needs to upgrade systems for existing purposes. The hotel will require further development of systems. There is a risk that until this is completed **data for local purposes** or for **central management review** will also be inadequate. It also may be difficult for central management to assess whether the **performance of the hotel is satisfactory** given that V cannot compare performance with other hotels that it owns. A further complication in assessment is whether management is prepared to **trade lower profitability** for the **increased assurance of quality** that owning and controlling its own hotel should bring.

Compensation risk

V will be **fully liable for any shortcomings in its own hotels** and will not be able to obtain the compensation that would have been available from the owners of the hotels that it has previously used. This may result in **increased costs**.

Answers   **133**

Property value risk

The hotel's value may fall due to, for example, **excessive wear and tear**, or a **collapse in local property prices** as a result of a fall in tourism or unstable local conditions.

Reputation risk

The new hotel poses a number of reputation risks for V. Firstly V's reputation will suffer if the hotel's opening is delayed and customers' **holidays have to be cancelled** or they are **switched to other hotels**. There is also the risk arising from the hotel gaining a bad reputation, either initially due to teething troubles or if there are subsequent problems. V can mitigate the risks arising from negative feedback when its customers use other owners' hotels by using different hotels in future. It will not be able to do that with a hotel that it owns itself.

(ii) **Control environment**

Legal expertise

V should consider recruiting **local expertise** to advise on, and assist in, managing the development process. A director should fly out to the country and establish relationships with local contacts. In particular **local legal advice** will be needed in connection with the property purchase and associated matters such as planning permission. Local legal advisers will also **play an important part in drawing up contracts with builders**. They should be recruited with a view to building a **longer-term relationship**, so that they can also provide advice on laws relating to the operation of the hotel.

Construction manager

The **time requirement** for overseeing the construction process on site will mean that it is unrealistic for a current director to be involved day-to-day. Instead a **local manager with experience of managing similar developments** should be recruited and report directly to V's main board.

Project team

A project team, headed by one of the **current directors** and including the **project manager** and a **senior member of the finance team**, also needs to oversee the project. The team needs to agree the **location and specification** for the hotel, and also set a **budget and a desired timescale** for the development.

Tendering

The project manager needs to **oversee a tendering process,** with several contractors being asked to tender and perhaps different contractors being used for different parts of the construction process. Contractors should provide **references** that should be checked. They should also provide **financial information** and other checks should be undertaken of their **financial stability** such as obtaining a **credit rating.**

Contracts

Establishing tight contracts with all the contractors chosen is the most important control. The contract details should include cost and timescale details. The system of **progress payments** should be made clear. There should be **penalty clauses** if contractors fail to complete on time due to matters that they are able to control. The contracts should also include provision for **rectification** by the contractors if their work is inadequate. The contract should give V the right of termination without penalty if a contractor's work is seriously flawed.

Reports

The local project manager should submit **regular reports** on the progress of the project to the project team and the director heading the team should in turn report to the main board. The reports should compare **actual progress with planned progress** and compare **budgeted cost** with **actual cost,** highlighting variances and explaining actions that will be taken to correct adverse variances. **Escalation triggers** also need to be built into the reporting, that immediate

reporting to project and board is required as soon as, for example, it appears that there will be delays above a certain length of time.

Site inspections

The project manager should be based at the site or make regular visits to the site. Other project team members should visit when **contract stages** are **completed** or when **progress payments** are due. The project manager should be allowed to recruit whatever **assistance** he needs to carry out an effective inspection of the work done.

Contingency plan

The project manager should establish a **contingency plan** for if the project falls behind timescale, or the builders go out of business or have to be taken off the contract, including possible alternative contractors.

(b)   (i)   **Cost of debt**

The indications are that the cost of debt is low. Although the **cost of equity** of V has not been calculated, there would be a cost attached to using the surplus funds, which is likely to be higher than the cost of debt, making this proposal potentially cheaper.

Availability of funds

The majority of V's cash at 30 June 2012 would be marked for the **dividend payment** of SK\$19.2m (SK\$24m x 0.8). The cash position will also reflect the money held in advance. Further cash will also be required in 2013 for the buyback of the Executive Chairman's shares. V is also examining other investment opportunities as well as an upgrade in information systems. It does not appear able to finance all these developments solely out of surplus cash and maintain dividend levels as well.

Debt capacity

V has the capacity under its current financing arrangements to take on **more debt**, up to a maximum of SK\$25 million, based on 2012 figures, although this will be lower if the share buyback take place.

Commitment to fixed costs

However, a commitment to pay interest will add to **V's fixed cost base.** As discussed above, V will be incurring additional fixed costs if it operates the hotel, which it may have trouble covering. Based on the 2012 accounts however, the extra finance cost should not be a particular problem as V's interest cover is nearly 10.

Matching of assets and liabilities

Taking out a **loan in regits** will be a way of hedging the risk of a fall in the value of the hotel due to adverse exchange rate movements. If the hotel's value falls in SK\$, the value of the loan will fall as well.

Matching of income and expenditure

The finance costs of the loan will however be an extra source of exchange risk, if the SK\$ weakens against the local currency in the country where the hotel is located. However V's **plans to attract local holidaymakers** will mitigate this risk, as it will be able to **match the contribution** in the local currency **against the expenditure.**

Repayment date

The loan would be repayable at the start of January 2023. This appears to fit in well with the other loans V currently has outstanding, with a 2.5 year gap between the repayment of the SK\$35m and the loan for the hotel. There should not be any liquidity problems through having to repay multiple sources of loan finance close together.

(ii) **Currency swap**

Time		Payment	Exchange rate	Discount factor	
		SK$/Rm		8%	SK$m
0	Principal	SK$6.000	5.000	1.000	6.000
1	Interest	R1.800	4.850	0.926	(0.344)
2	Interest	R1.800	4.705	0.857	(0.328)
3	Interest	R1.800	4.563	0.794	(0.313)
4	Interest	R1.800	4.426	0.735	(0.299)
5	Interest	R1.800	4.294	0.681	(0.285)
6	Interest	R1.800	4.165	0.630	(0.272)
7	Interest	R1.800	4.040	0.583	(0.260)
8	Interest	R1.800	3.919	0.540	(0.248)
9	Interest	R1.800	3.801	0.500	(0.237)
10	Interest plus Principal	R31.800	3.687	0.463	(3.993)
	Present value				(0.579)

The negative figure suggests that the swap may not be accepted. The negative figure results from the depreciation of the SK$.

(c) **Low customer take-up**

Customers may not think that the amounts charged for the premium, all-inclusive deals represent good value and may go elsewhere.

The risk can be **monitored** by **continuous review** of the number of holidays booked and total revenue, and also **measures of customer satisfaction** through focus groups, questionnaires and external sources such as trade reports. The risk can be **limited by marketing activity** that targets likely customers, such as customers who have bought all-inclusive deals from V for other resorts, and sets out the services and the quality offered in the all-inclusive package, so that customers are well-informed of what V is offering. V should investigate through **market research** offering (and marketing) extra benefits in the package over time to maintain and increase its **differentiation** from competitors.

Failure to cover costs

Given the nature of the market, it is unlikely that V will be able to **obtain full revenues** on all the inclusive holidays it sells. However, unsold holidays increase the risk that fixed costs won't be covered.

V can **monitor the threat** of cut-price holidays by maintaining awareness of the **deals being offered by competitors** and also **take-up of its own packages.** V can **limit the risk** by developing its system for offering discounts, bringing in **flexibility** to the deals it offers that depends on time of booking. Last minute deals will be worthwhile for V if the income makes a positive contribution, but V needs to review what is offered on-line and at branches, in order to ensure it is not offering generous discounts too early when it could still be selling full-price holidays.

Excessive costs

The all-inclusive deals offered may mean a risk of significant costs arising from customers eating and drinking **excessive amounts**. Ultimately the income received may not cover the costs of supplying them. V has not previously incurred this risk directly because it has not owned the hotels it has used.

Expenditure and consumption of each category of food and drink consumable needs to be **budgeted, actual figures compared and variances highlighted**. V can **limit the risk** by **control over the portion sizes** that are given to customers, or **providing buffets** which customers are only allowed to visit once each meal. Controlling drinking may be more difficult, and perhaps can be best achieved by **limiting bar opening hours**.

Theft by staff

V faces the risk of losses through theft by staff of inventory. This risk is difficult to monitor as the all-inclusive nature of the package means that **consumption is not directly matched with cash receipts**.

Again **monitoring consumption** of **each category** of food and drink might highlight problems. V can **limit the risk by limiting access to inventory** to certain individuals, and **obtaining references** for staff who are in positions of trust. **Recording customer orders and matching these with consumption** would be a substitute for not being able to match with cash receipts. Limited internal audit work, particularly surprise visits to count inventory and reconcile with records, should help reduce the risk.

(d) Complaints/poor ratings

Perhaps the most obvious source of deciding which representatives to investigate further is **complaints or poor ratings** by customers, either to V directly or from other sources, for example well-known online forums such as Tripadvisor. Measurement of customer satisfaction needs to **include a grading system**, to enable comparison of the performance of different representatives. However, where staff have **consistently achieved poor ratings** or there are **well-substantiated complaints**, HR action, such as a performance improvement programme or dismissal, needs to be taken quickly rather than waiting for the representative' s performance to be assessed by auditors.

New staff

New representatives clearly represent a **relatively high risk** for V. They may take some time to receive all the training that they require. If they are **new to the industry**, it will also take time for them to gain experience of dealing with a variety of different problems. In addition, sufficient data on their performance through the customer feedback system may take **time to emerge** and V would want to identify problems with their performance early on.

HR issues

Staff's HR records are also a source of evidence that may determine which staff re selected. One indication of higher risk would be where staff's line managers had raised concerns about **aspects of their performance**. Less reliable indicators, but ones which auditors should consider, are where staff have made complaints that may indicate poor staff motivation and hence indicate a risk of poor performance. These include complaints about pay, working conditions or issues in dealing with V's systems. Auditors may also be particularly concerned if staff had made **complaints** that did not appear to have been adequately resolved.

Supervision of staff

HR records might also indicate which staff had been **inadequately supervised**. Hence an internal audit visit would be needed to compensate for a failure of line management. Evidence of inadequate supervision would include **failure to carry out appraisals**, to **visit staff on-site** or to **respond adequately to complaints** that had been made about staff.

Analytical reviews of expenses

Analytical procedures can be used to indicate excessive expenditure by representatives. Auditors can use them to identify whether expenditure levels are **in accordance with their expectations**. Comparisons can be made over **time and in the light of local costs. Comparisons can also be made with other representatives** as auditors would expect the levels of certain types of expenditure to be reasonably consistent. Analytical procedures may be particularly useful for highlighting queries over expenditure where reliable documentation would normally be lacking.

Documentation of expenses

Auditors should also review centrally-available documentation of the representatives' expenses to see if there were any **unusual features**, for example use of an unexpected supplier. They would be more concerned if centrally-available documentation was lacking, or the representative's line manager or other staff had raised concerns about **inadequate documentation.** Again though, if the evidence clearly indicated a serious problem, the issue ought probably to be **addressed immediately** by the representative's manager as an internal audit visit may not provide much extra information.

MATHEMATICAL TABLES
AND FORMULAE

MATHEMATICAL TABLES AND FORMULAE

AREA UNDER THE NORMAL CURVE

This table gives the area under the normal curve between the mean and a point Z standard deviations above the mean. The corresponding area for deviations below the mean can be found by symmetry.

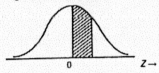

$Z = \dfrac{(x - \mu)}{\sigma}$	0.00	0.01	0.02	0.03	0.04	0.05	0.06	0.07	0.08	0.09
0.0	.0000	.0040	.0080	.0120	.0159	.0199	.0239	.0279	.0319	.0359
0.1	.0398	.0438	.0478	.0517	.0557	.0596	.0636	.0675	.0714	.0753
0.2	.0793	.0832	.0871	.0910	.0948	.0987	.1026	.1064	.1103	.1141
0.3	.1179	.1217	.1255	.1293	.1331	.1368	.1406	.1443	.1480	.1517
0.4	.1554	.1591	.1628	.1664	.1700	.1736	.1772	.1808	.1844	.1879
0.5	.1915	.1950	.1985	.2019	.2054	.2088	.2123	.2157	.2190	.2224
0.6	.2257	.2291	.2324	.2357	.2389	.2422	.2454	.2486	.2518	.2549
0.7	.2580	.2611	.2642	.2673	.2704	.2734	.2764	.2794	.2823	.2852
0.8	.2881	.2910	.2939	.2967	.2995	.3023	.3051	.3078	.3106	.3133
0.9	.3159	.3186	.3212	.3238	.3264	.3289	.3315	.3340	.3365	.3389
1.0	.3413	.3438	.3461	.3485	.3508	.3531	.3554	.3577	.3599	.3621
1.1	.3643	.3665	.3686	.3708	.3729	.3749	.3770	.3790	.3810	.3830
1.2	.3849	.3869	.3888	.3907	.3925	.3944	.3962	.3980	.3997	.4015
1.3	.4032	.4049	.4066	.4082	.4099	.4115	.4131	.4147	.4162	.4177
1.4	.4192	.4207	.4222	.4236	.4251	.4265	.4279	.4292	.4306	.4319
1.5	.4332	.4345	.4357	.4370	.4382	.4394	.4406	.4418	.4430	.4441
1.6	.4452	.4463	.4474	.4485	.4495	.4505	.4515	.4525	.4535	.4545
1.7	.4554	.4564	.4573	.4582	.4591	.4599	.4608	.4616	.4625	.4633
1.8	.4641	.4649	.4656	.4664	.4671	.4678	.4686	.4693	.4699	.4706
1.9	.4713	.4719	.4726	.4732	.4738	.4744	.4750	.4756	.4762	.4767
2.0	.4772	.4778	.4783	.4788	.4793	.4798	.4803	.4808	.4812	.4817
2.1	.4821	.4826	.4830	.4834	.4838	.4842	.4846	.4850	.4854	.4857
2.2	.4861	.4865	.4868	.4871	.4875	.4878	.4881	.4884	.4887	.4890
2.3	.4893	.4896	.4898	.4901	.4904	.4906	.4909	.4911	.4913	.4916
2.4	.4918	.4920	.4922	.4925	.4927	.4929	.4931	.4932	.4934	.4936
2.5	.4938	.4940	.4941	.4943	.4945	.4946	.4948	.4949	.4951	.4952
2.6	.4953	.4955	.4956	.4957	.4959	.4960	.4961	.4962	.4963	.4964
2.7	.4965	.4966	.4967	.4968	.4969	.4970	.4971	.4972	.4973	.4974
2.8	.4974	.4975	.4976	.4977	.4977	.4978	.4979	.4980	.4980	.4981
2.9	.4981	.4982	.4983	.4983	.4984	.4984	.4985	.4985	.4986	.4986
3.0	.49865	.4987	.4987	.4988	.4988	.4989	.4989	.4989	.4990	.4990
3.1	.49903	.4991	.4991	.4991	.4992	.4992	.4992	.4992	.4993	.4993
3.2	.49931	.4993	.4994	.4994	.4994	.4994	.4994	.4995	.4995	.4995
3.3	.49952	.4995	.4995	.4996	.4996	.4996	.4996	.4996	.4996	.4997
3.4	.49966	.4997	.4997	.4997	.4997	.4997	.4997	.4997	.4997	.4998
3.5	.49977									

PRESENT VALUE TABLE

Present value of 1.00 unit of currency ie $(1+r)^{-n}$ where r = interest rate, n = number of periods until payment or receipt.

Periods	Interest rates (r)									
(n)	1%	2%	3%	4%	5%	6%	7%	8%	9%	10%
1	0.990	0.980	0.971	0.962	0.952	0.943	0.935	0.926	0.917	0.909
2	0.980	0.961	0.943	0.925	0.907	0.890	0.873	0.857	0.842	0.826
3	0.971	0.942	0.915	0.889	0.864	0.840	0.816	0.794	0.772	0.751
4	0.961	0.924	0.888	0.855	0.823	0.792	0.763	0.735	0.708	0.683
5	0.951	0.906	0.863	0.822	0.784	0.747	0.713	0.681	0.650	0.621
6	0.942	0.888	0.837	0.790	0.746	0705	0.666	0.630	0.596	0.564
7	0.933	0.871	0.813	0.760	0.711	0.665	0.623	0.583	0.547	0.513
8	0.923	0.853	0.789	0.731	0.677	0.627	0.582	0.540	0.502	0.467
9	0.914	0.837	0.766	0.703	0.645	0.592	0.544	0.500	0.460	0.424
10	0.905	0.820	0.744	0.676	0.614	0.558	0.508	0.463	0.422	0.386
11	0.896	0.804	0.722	0.650	0.585	0.527	0.475	0.429	0.388	0.350
12	0.887	0.788	0.701	0.625	0.557	0.497	0.444	0.397	0.356	0.319
13	0.879	0.773	0.681	0.601	0.530	0.469	0.415	0.368	0.326	0.290
14	0.870	0.758	0.661	0.577	0.505	0.442	0.388	0.340	0.299	0.263
15	0.861	0.743	0.642	0.555	0.481	0.417	0.362	0.315	0.275	0.239
16	0.853	0.728	0.623	0.534	0.458	0.394	0.339	0.292	0.252	0.218
17	0.844	0.714	0.605	0.513	0.436	0.371	0.317	0.270	0.231	0.198
18	0.836	0.700	0.587	0.494	0.416	0.350	0.296	0.250	0.212	0.180
19	0.828	0.686	0.570	0.475	0.396	0.331	0.277	0.232	0.194	0.164
20	0.820	0.673	0.554	0.456	0.377	0.312	0.258	0.215	0.178	0.149

Periods	Interest rates (r)									
(n)	11%	12%	13%	14%	15%	16%	17%	18%	19%	20%
1	0.901	0.893	0.885	0.877	0.870	0.862	0.855	0.847	0.840	0.833
2	0.812	0.797	0.783	0.769	0.756	0.743	0.731	0.718	0.706	0.694
3	0.731	0.712	0.693	0.675	0.658	0.641	0.624	0.609	0.593	0.579
4	0.659	0.636	0.613	0.592	0.572	0.552	0.534	0.516	0.499	0.482
5	0.593	0.567	0.543	0.519	0.497	0.476	0.456	0.437	0.419	0.402
6	0.535	0.507	0.480	0.456	0.432	0.410	0.390	0.370	0.352	0.335
7	0.482	0.452	0.425	0.400	0.376	0.354	0.333	0.314	0.296	0.279
8	0.434	0.404	0.376	0.351	0.327	0.305	0.285	0.266	0.249	0.233
9	0.391	0.361	0.333	0.308	0.284	0.263	0.243	0.225	0.209	0.194
10	0.352	0.322	0.295	0.270	0.247	0.227	0.208	0.191	0.176	0.162
11	0.317	0.287	0.261	0.237	0.215	0.195	0.178	0.162	0.148	0.135
12	0.286	0.257	0.231	0.208	0.187	0.168	0.152	0.137	0.124	0.112
13	0.258	0.229	0.204	0.182	0.163	0.145	0.130	0.116	0.104	0.093
14	0.232	0.205	0.181	0.160	0.141	0.125	0.111	0.099	0.088	0.078
15	0.209	0.183	0.160	0.140	0.123	0.108	0.095	0.084	0.079	0.065
16	0.188	0.163	0.141	0.123	0.107	0.093	0.081	0.071	0.062	0.054
17	0.170	0.146	0.125	0.108	0.093	0.080	0.069	0.060	0.052	0.045
18	0.153	0.130	0.111	0.095	0.081	0.069	0.059	0.051	0.044	0.038
19	0.138	0.116	0.098	0.083	0.070	0.060	0.051	0.043	0.037	0.031
20	0.124	0.104	0.087	0.073	0.061	0.051	0.043	0.037	0.031	0.026

CUMULATIVE PRESENT VALUE TABLE

This table shows the present value of 1.00 unit of currency per annum, receivable or payable at the end of each year for n years $\dfrac{1-(1+r)^{-n}}{r}$.

Periods	Interest rates (r)									
(n)	1%	2%	3%	4%	5%	6%	7%	8%	9%	10%
1	0.990	0.980	0.971	0.962	0.952	0.943	0.935	0.926	0.917	0.909
2	1.970	1.942	1.913	1.886	1.859	1.833	1.808	1.783	1.759	1.736
3	2.941	2.884	2.829	2.775	2.723	2.673	2.624	2.577	2.531	2.487
4	3.902	3.808	3.717	3.630	3.546	3.465	3.387	3.312	3.240	3.170
5	4.853	4.713	4.580	4.452	4.329	4.212	4.100	3.993	3.890	3.791
6	5.795	5.601	5.417	5.242	5.076	4.917	4.767	4.623	4.486	4.355
7	6.728	6.472	6.230	6.002	5.786	5.582	5.389	5.206	5.033	4.868
8	7.652	7.325	7.020	6.733	6.463	6.210	5.971	5.747	5.535	5.335
9	8.566	8.162	7.786	7.435	7.108	6.802	6.515	6.247	5.995	5.759
10	9.471	8.983	8.530	8.111	7.722	7.360	7.024	6.710	6.418	6.145
11	10.368	9.787	9.253	8.760	8.306	7.887	7.499	7.139	6.805	6.495
12	11.255	10.575	9.954	9.385	8.863	8.384	7.943	7.536	7.161	6.814
13	12.134	11.348	10.635	9.986	9.394	8.853	8.358	7.904	7.487	7.103
14	13.004	12.106	11.296	10.563	9.899	9.295	8.745	8.244	7.786	7.367
15	13.865	12.849	11.938	11.118	10.380	9.712	9.108	8.559	8.061	7.606
16	14.718	13.578	12.561	11.652	10.838	10.106	9.447	8.851	8.313	7.824
17	15.562	14.292	13.166	12.166	11.274	10.477	9.763	9.122	8.544	8.022
18	16.398	14.992	13.754	12.659	11.690	10.828	10.059	9.372	8.756	8.201
19	17.226	15.679	14.324	13.134	12.085	11.158	10.336	9.604	8.950	8.365
20	18.046	16.351	14.878	13.590	12.462	11.470	10.594	9.818	9.129	8.514

Periods	Interest rates (r)									
(n)	11%	12%	13%	14%	15%	16%	17%	18%	19%	20%
1	0.901	0.893	0.885	0.877	0.870	0.862	0.855	0.847	0.840	0.833
2	1.713	1.690	1.668	1.647	1.626	1.605	1.585	1.566	1.547	1.528
3	2.444	2.402	2.361	2.322	2.283	2.246	2.210	2.174	2.140	2.106
4	3.102	3.037	2.974	2.914	2.855	2.798	2.743	2.690	2.639	2.589
5	3.696	3.605	3.517	3.433	3.352	3.274	3.199	3.127	3.058	2.991
6	4.231	4.111	3.998	3.889	3.784	3.685	3.589	3.498	3.410	3.326
7	4.712	4.564	4.423	4.288	4.160	4.039	3.922	3.812	3.706	3.605
8	5.146	4.968	4.799	4.639	4.487	4.344	4.207	4.078	3.954	3.837
9	5.537	5.328	5.132	4.946	4.772	4.607	4.451	4.303	4.163	4.031
10	5.889	5.650	5.426	5.216	5.019	4.833	4.659	4.494	4.339	4.192
11	6.207	5.938	5.687	5.453	5.234	5.029	4.836	4.656	4.486	4.327
12	6.492	6.194	5.918	5.660	5.421	5.197	4.988	7.793	4.611	4.439
13	6.750	6.424	6.122	5.842	5.583	5.342	5.118	4.910	4.715	4.533
14	6.982	6.628	6.302	6.002	5.724	5.468	5.229	5.008	4.802	4.611
15	7.191	6.811	6.462	6.142	5.847	5.575	5.324	5.092	4.876	4.675
16	7.379	6.974	6.604	6.265	5.954	5.668	5.405	5.162	4.938	4.730
17	7.549	7.120	6.729	6.373	6.047	5.749	5.475	5.222	4.990	4.775
18	7.702	7.250	6.840	6.467	6.128	5.818	5.534	5.273	5.033	4.812
19	7.839	7.366	6.938	6.550	6.198	5.877	5.584	5.316	5.070	4.843
20	7.963	7.469	7.025	6.623	6.259	5.929	5.628	5.353	5.101	4.870

EXAM FORMULAE

Annuity

Present value of an annuity of £1 per annum receivable or payable for n years, commencing in one year, discounted at r% per annum:

$$PV = \frac{1}{r}\left[1 - \frac{1}{[1+r]^n}\right]$$

Perpetuity

Present value of £1 per annum, payable or receivable in perpetuity, commencing in one year, discounted at r% per annum:

$$PV = \frac{1}{r}$$

Growing Perpetuity

Present value of £1 per annum, receivable or payable, commencing in one year, growing in perpetuity at a constant rate of g% per annum, discounted at r% per annum:

$$PV = \frac{1}{r-g}$$